RICHARD M. NARDONE

The Story of the Christian Year

PAULIST PRESS
New York/Mahwah, N.J.

Maps by Frank Sabatté, C.S.P.

Library of Congress Cataloging-in-Publication Data

Nardone, Richard M., 1929–
    The story of the Christian year/Richard M. Nardone.
      p. cm.
    Includes bibliographical references.
    ISBN 0-8091-3277-X (pb.)
    1. Church year—History. I. Title.
  BV30.N37   1991
  263'.9'09—dc20   91-31717
                                                      CIP

Published by Paulist Press
997 Macarthur Boulevard
Mahwah, New Jersey 07430

Printed and bound in the United States of America

Contents

115804

To Marianne

Abbreviations

AAS   *Acta Apostolicae Sedis* (Rome, 1909–).

ANF   *The Ante-Nicene Fathers,* 10 vols. (Buffalo, 1884–1897).

EL   *Epheremides Liturgicae* (Rome, 1887–).

NPNF   *The Nicene and Post-Nicene Fathers,* Series I and II, 28 vols. (Buffalo & New York, 1886–1900).

PL   *Patrologia Latina,* ed. J.P. Migne, 221 vols. (Paris, 1844–1864).

SC   *Sources chrétiennes* (Paris, 1941–).

Preface

Edmund Bishop, in his famous essay on the genius of the Roman rite, listed these characteristics: "simplicity, practicality, a great sobriety and self-control, gravity and dignity." For the Roman Christians of the second century, the Christian year consisted of the Sunday eucharist and little if anything else. Even the feast of Easter was accepted in Rome with a certain reluctance, and only on condition that it be celebrated on Sunday, when people would be going to mass anyway. And when they did go to mass, their prayers were very short and very practical: "O God, whose providence never fails, hear our prayers. Deliver us from all things harmful and provide for all our needs." That was the prayer for the seventh Sunday after Pentecost, now read on the ninth Sunday in Ordinary Time.

If the Romans had been left alone, they would probably have kept their worship unchanged down through the centuries. In the words of Cardinal Newman: "Rome, except in the case of some great popes, has never shown any great gift of origination." A Roman would take that as a compliment. But of course they were not left alone. The Byzantine church and empire contributed new feast days and a more elaborate ceremonial. Some of the clergy even took to wearing stoles, to distinguish themselves from the laity. They were told to wear them under their coats (chasubles), where they wouldn't be seen. Pope Celestine I sternly reminded them that the clergy should be distinguished from the laity "by our learning, not by our dress, by our life, not by our robes."

After the Greeks came the Franks and the Germans. They added new ceremonies to the Holy Week services (the Romans had been content with Bible readings). They had the Creed recited at mass. They gave the church new feast days, e.g. Corpus Christi and Trinity Sunday. And after the Franks and Germans came the religious orders. They gave the church many new saints and many new devotions, e.g. the Holy Name of Jesus, the Sacred Heart of Jesus, Our Lady of the Rosary, Our Lady of Mount Carmel, Our Lady of Mercy.

Rome usually resisted at first, but eventually gave in. As Pope Stephen I put it in the third century, "Nihil innovetur nisi quod traditum est" (No innovations; follow tradition). Or in the words of the Second Vatican Council, "There must be no innovations unless the good of the church genuinely and certainly requires them."

For the opportunity to tell this story, I am deeply grateful to Paulist Press and to Seton Hall University.

ONE

The Early Christian Church

The New Testament

Anyone looking in the New Testament for the origin of the Christian holy days will be disappointed, because there is very little information about early Christian worship. We have the teaching of Jesus about prayer, and two versions of the Lord's Prayer (Mt 6:5–15; Lk 11:1–13). We have the commandment to preach the gospel and to baptize those who believe (Mt 28:18–20; Mk 16:15–18). And we have the story of the Lord's supper and the command to "do this in memory of me" (Mt 26:26–30; Mk 14:22–26; Lk 22:14–20). But St. Paul never mentions the Lord's supper in his letters except in 1 Corinthians 11:17–34, and that was only by accident, because of the abuses he wanted to condemn in the church of Corinth. Even so, we have to wait a hundred years longer before finding an actual description of the eucharist.

The Christians gathered together for worship, not on the Jewish sabbath (Saturday, the seventh day of the week), but on Sunday, the first day of the week, the day of the Lord's resurrection. The gospel stories of the resurrection make a special point of noting that it took place on a Sunday (Mt 28:1; Mk 16:2; Lk 24:1; Jn 20:1). Later that same day, according to Luke, Jesus appeared to two of his disciples, and at supper he took bread, and blessed it, and broke it, and gave it to them (24:30), and still later that day he appeared to the disciples in Jerusalem (24:36). Therefore the Lord's supper, which Luke calls the "breaking of the bread," is associated with the resur-

3

rection even on the first Easter Sunday. And according to John, the very next Sunday was marked by an assembly of the Lord's disciples and by another appearance of the risen Christ (20:26).

St. Paul's reference to the eucharist in 1 Corinthians 11 does not include any information about when it was celebrated, but at the end of the letter he tells them to take up a special collection every Sunday for the mother church in Jerusalem (16:2), which indicates clearly enough that Sunday was their day of worship. In the Acts of the Apostles, we are told that St. Paul preached at great length in the city of Troas, "on the first day of the week, when we gathered to break bread" (20:7). His sermon lasted until midnight, which reminds us that the eucharist was originally celebrated in the evening, at a real supper. But the complaint of St. Paul about the behavior of the Christians in Corinth ("one goes hungry while another gets drunk") shows why the church moved the eucharist to the morning, as a general rule, separating it from the agape, or love feast. The evening love feasts remained popular, but after the fourth century they gradually died out.

In the book of Revelation (Apocalypse), the author's vision took place on "the Lord's day," the new Christian name for Sunday (1:10). It became the Lord's day not only in Greek but also in Latin and the Romance languages, although the pagan name of Sunday survived in English and the other Germanic languages.

It should be clear that the Christian Sunday, as the weekly memorial of Christ's resurrection, was quite distinct from the Jewish sabbath. It seems that the original Jewish Christians continued to observe the sabbath in some fashion, to which they added the observance of the Lord's supper on Sunday. The sabbath law was not binding on Gentile Christians (Acts 15:28–29), but St. Paul had to defend their freedom against the efforts of the Judaizers: "Let no one, then, pass judgment on you in matters of food and drink or with regard to a festival or new moon or sabbath" (Col 2:16; cf. Gal 4:10; Rom 14:5). Certainly there was no attempt to transfer the day of rest from Saturday to Sunday. At least until the fourth century, Sunday was an ordinary working day for pagans and Christians alike, with the eucharist celebrated in the early morning, like the modern weekday masses.

There is at least this connection between the Jewish sabbath and the Christian Sunday, that they were both *weekly* holy days. The seven day week was of vital importance in Judaism, of course, but it also figured in pagan astrology in which each day was dedicated to its governing planet. Ordinarily, however, pagan feast days were celebrated on an annual, not a weekly, basis. In pagan society people needed to know what day of the month it was, but there was little, if any, need to know what day of the week it was. The weekly Lord's day of the Christians, therefore, shows the influence of Judaism. For a different reason, the Jewish calendar would also be followed in the whole Easter cycle of movable holy days, while the fixed holy days would follow the Roman calendar.

The Second Century

Outside the New Testament, the oldest reference to the Christian Sunday would seem to be in the *Didache,* which may date from the first century: "On the Lord's day come together, break bread and give thanks [or celebrate the eucharist], after confessing your sins so that your sacrifice may be pure."[1] The Lord's supper is now called the thanksgiving (eucharist in Greek), and it is regarded as the Christian sacrifice foretold by the prophet Malachi, who is quoted in the following sentence: "In every place and time offer me a pure sacrifice" (Mal 1:11).

In the early years of the second century, St. Ignatius of Antioch described Christians as "no longer keeping the sabbath but living according to the Lord's day."[2] And in the Letter of Barnabas we find the first reference to Sunday as the eighth day, that is, as a new beginning, a new creation: "Therefore we celebrate with joy the eighth day on which Jesus rose from the dead, and was made manifest and ascended into heaven."[3] Also dating from this period is the letter of Pliny the Younger, governor of Bithynia, to the emperor Trajan. He reported that the Christians assembled before daybreak on an appointed day, when they sang hymns to Christ as to a god, and they met again later in the day for a meal.[4] These Christians were sentenced to death, unless they recanted.

The *Apology* of St. Justin Martyr (c. A.D. 150) has the oldest description of the eucharist.[5] Since he was writing for pagan readers, he used terminology they would understand. He told them that the Christians celebrated the eucharist "on the day of the sun," because on that day God created the universe, and on that same day Christ rose from the dead.[6] In his *Dialogue with Trypho the Jew,* Justin admits that Christians do not keep the Jewish law, and they are not circumcised, and they do not observe the sabbath.[7] Then, quoting the prophet Malachi, he speaks of the Christian sacrifice as the bread and cup of the eucharist, and the day of Christ's resurrection he calls the first day, which is also the eighth day, the day after the sabbath.[8]

In addition to the Sunday eucharist, the *Didache* also witnesses to two other primitive customs. Christians are told to fast on Wednesdays and Fridays, and not on the Jewish fast days of Monday and Thursday. No reason is given. And they are also told to recite the Lord's Prayer three times a day (the text of the Lord's Prayer is given, ending with a doxology).[9]

The Development of Easter

Easter, the annual feast of Christ's resurrection, is certainly very ancient, but it may not go back to the very beginning of the church. There is no mention of it in the New Testament. But the feast of the Passover (*Pascha*) and the Unleavened Bread was given a new meaning. According to St. Paul, "Christ, our paschal lamb, has been sacrificed. Therefore, let us celebrate the feast, not with the old yeast, the yeast of malice and wickedness, but with the unleavened bread of sincerity and truth" (1 Cor 5:7–8). For Christians, therefore, Christ is "the lamb of God, who takes away the sin of the world" (Jn 1:29).[10] But when this belief was expressed in a Christian Passover feast, it led to controversy.

The story of the Easter controversy is told in the *Church History* of Eusebius of Caesarea.[11] In the second century the churches in Asia Minor celebrated a paschal feast, preceded by a fast, on the same day as the Jewish Passover, that is, on 14 Nisan. They claimed that this "quartodeciman" (or "fourteenth") date had apostolic authority. But the other Christian churches celebrated Easter on the following Sunday. It is possible that the Roman church, always very conservative, did not celebrate Easter at all. Actually, since *every* Sunday was a memorial of the resurrection, Easter Sunday would differ from the others only in the preceding fast, and this controversy was about the fast as well as the feast. When St. Polycarp of Smyrna visited Rome in the time of Pope Anicetus (c. 155–166), the two bishops disagreed on this question, but remained in communion with one another.

While it is not clear whether the Roman church celebrated Easter at all in the days of Anicetus, by the time of Pope Victor (189–199) the feast was being kept on Sunday and this was now the general custom throughout the Catholic Church. It was preceded by at least one day of fasting. Victor then threatened to excommunicate the Quartodecimans if they did not celebrate Easter with the rest of the Christian world, but they refused to do so, and Victor himself was rebuked by his fellow bishops. They did not think the question was that important. Ultimately, of course, all the churches agreed to celebrate Easter on Sunday.

When the paschal feast was kept on the same day as the Jewish Passover, the emphasis would have been on the death of Christ, while the Sunday observance would emphasize the Lord's resurrection. But actually both the death and the resurrection were part of the one paschal mystery in both cases. In the *Paschal Homily* of Melito of Sardis (who happened to be one of the Quartodeciman bishops), the oldest such homily in existence, the paschal mystery embraces the whole story of our salvation.[12] It is the memorial of the Lord's birth in time, his death and burial, his resurrection and ascension, and the expectation of his coming again to judge the living and the dead. These different aspects of the one paschal feast would later become separate feast days, but Easter would always remain "the most solemn of all feasts."[13]

Both in Greek and in Latin, this festival is called the *Pascha,* the Passover, and this name has been retained in the various Romance languages and in some Germanic languages. The derivation of Easter, the English name for the feast, is a matter of dispute.[14] The Venerable Bede thought it was the name of a pre-Christian goddess of spring, but that seems to be doubtful.[15]

Even when the Christian world agreed that Easter should be celebrated on a Sunday, there still remained the problem of determining the date in advance. The Jewish Passover was celebrated on the first full moon after the spring equinox, and Easter should fall on the following Sunday, but both Christians and Jews found it difficult to do the necessary calculations. The Council of Nicaea (A.D. 325) tried to impose a single system to be followed by all the churches, but it was only in the sixth century that a more or less general agreement was reached. The Celtic churches, however, continued to follow their own system until the eighth century.[16] The tables for finding the date of Easter in any given year were printed in the Roman Missal right down to the Second Vatican Council, although they were seldom, if ever, used. It was much easier to consult the list of years with the date of Easter printed alongside. Even today some churches, mainly Eastern Orthodox, still use the Julian calendar instead of the Gregorian calendar adopted in 1582, and that can affect the date of Easter, since the spring equinox in the Julian calendar is about two weeks later than the Gregorian date.

By the end of the second century, the initiation rite of baptism had become associated with the Easter festival, at least in some places. In North Africa Tertullian thought that Easter was the most suitable time for baptism, and, after that, Pentecost, that is, the "fifty days" after Easter. But he adds that "every day is the Lord's; every hour, every time, is suitable for baptism."[17] In Rome, according to the *Apostolic Tradition* of St. Hippolytus, there was a vigil on Saturday night ending with the baptismal rite early on Sunday morning, and then the eucharist. But the Sunday in question was not necessarily Easter Sunday.[18] Certainly by the fourth century, in Rome and in most other places, Easter Sunday had become the principal day for baptisms. In Alexandria, however, it seems that Easter baptisms only date from the year 385, under Bishop Theophilus.[19] Since the rite was intended primarily for adult converts, when all of pagan society became Christian it was replaced by the private baptism of infants right after birth.

The Veneration of the Saints

Although Easter was the only annual festival of the whole Christian world, the veneration of the saints on a local basis can be traced back to the second century. Bishop Polycarp of Smyrna suffered martyrdom on February 23, 155 or 156, and an account of his martyrdom was written by his community.[20] They called him a "wonderful martyr" and an "apostolic and prophetic teacher and bishop of the Catholic Church in Smyrna." And they promised to meet at his tomb for a memorial service on the anniversary of his death. Originally these honors were reserved for the martyrs, and there would be a great multitude of martyrs during the following centuries. Normally it would be a strictly local celebration, at the very tomb of the martyr. But when the persecutions ended in the fourth century, these liturgical honors were extended to other saintly men and women, and the more popular saints were venerated, not just locally, but in all the churches.

Daily Prayer

The primitive instruction to say the Lord's Prayer three times a day, as found in the *Didache,* would later be expanded into whole treatises on prayer. Tertullian, for example, thought that Christians should pray always and everywhere, since that was the teaching of Jesus (Lk 18:1) and St. Paul (Eph 6:18; Col 4:2; 1 Thess 5:17; 1 Tim 2:8).[21] But he mentioned the special importance of praying at the third, sixth, and ninth hours of the day (roughly 9 a.m., 12 noon, and 3 p.m.), in addition to the usual morning and evening prayers, which were regarded as obligatory.[22] The very practical reason for choosing these times, as Tertullian admits elsewhere, was that they marked the familiar divisions of the business day.[23] But it was easy enough to find various biblical texts that would give a religious meaning to these hours of prayer. Both Tertullian and Origen of Alexandria mention the prophet Daniel, who prayed three times a day (Dan 6:11).[24] And the psalmist also prayed "in the evening, and at dawn, and at noon" (Ps 55:18).

It was not so important to find a scriptural basis for morning and evening prayer, since those hours were traditional anyway, but the three additional hours were not so well established. In the Acts of the Apostles, Tertullian found that the Holy Spirit descended on the apostles at the third hour, St. Peter's vision at Joppa was at the sixth hour, and Peter and John cured the man crippled from birth as they were going into the temple to pray at the ninth hour (Acts 2:15; 10:9; 3:1). And so he could claim that prayer at those hours was an apostolic tradition, not to mention the trinitarian symbolism of the number three.

Tertullian was also aware of another reason for praying at the three hours, the reason given in the *Apostolic Tradition* of St. Hippolytus.[25] These were the hours of the Lord's passion in the gospel of Mark, in which Jesus is crucified at the third hour, darkness falls at the sixth hour, and Jesus dies at the ninth hour (Mk 15:25, 33–34). Hippolytus also mentioned the duty of praying when rising in the morning and when retiring at night, but like Tertullian he did not bother to look for biblical texts for those hours.

Besides praying at intervals during the day, Christians were also expected to pray during the night. Origen appealed to the example of the psalmist: "At midnight I rise to give you thanks" (Ps 119:62).[26] And Hippolytus gave as one reason the tradition that all creation pauses at midnight to praise the Lord, and as another reason the parable of the ten virgins: "At midnight there was a cry, 'Behold the bridegroom! Come out to meet him!' . . . Therefore stay awake, for you know neither the day nor the hour" (Mt 25:6, 13). Actually Hippolytus wanted Christians to pray twice during the night, once at midnight and again at cockcrow.[27] Later in the third century, St. Cyprian of Carthage, after explaining the reasons for prayer at the three hours of the day, and in the morning and evening, also urges his people to pray during the night like the widow Anna, who "never left the temple, but worshiped night and day with fasting and prayer" (Lk 2:37).[28]

Normally these daily prayers would be said privately. But in the *Apostolic Tradition* the faithful are urged to go to the place of assembly whenever an instruction is given in the word of God.[29] This instruction is distinct from the regular Sunday eucharist, and like the eucharist was held early in the morning. On the days when there was no instruction, the faithful were advised to spend the time in spiritual reading at home.[30] Apparently there were no evening services except for the occasional *agape,* or love feast, which included the ceremony of the *lucernarium,* or lamp-lighting, at the beginning of the supper.[31]

The general picture that emerges for this period shows us a community gathered together every Sunday to celebrate the eucharist, and praying frequently during the week. They fasted twice a week, on Wednesdays and Fridays. The annual Easter festival was an early, if not primitive, development, and was probably the only annual feast celebrated by the whole church. The anniversaries of the martyrs were still local observances at their tombs. But the victory of the church over paganism in the fourth century would affect the church's worship, for better or for worse.

How Liturgies Evolve

Before moving on to the next period, it might be useful to review the "laws of liturgical evolution" formulated by Anton Baumstark.[32] In the chapters that follow, we will see further how these laws govern the evolution of the liturgy.

(1) There is an evolution from variety to uniformity. The usages of the great churches would be adopted, more or less willingly, by the lesser churches. In that way the Roman rite prevailed in the west, and the rites of Constantinople, Antioch, Alexandria, and Jerusalem in the east. Eventually the Orthodox Church would impose the Byzantine rite of Constantinople on all the Orthodox churches. In the Catholic Church, however, the Roman rite co-exists with other rites even today.

(2) There is an evolution from simplicity to richness. So, for example, the introit and gradual psalms of the old Roman mass were replaced by a verse or two sung to an elaborate melody. The bringing of the bread and wine to the altar developed into the great entrance of the Byzantine liturgy. And the few feasts of local martyrs gave way to an overloaded calendar of saints.

(3) There is an evolution from freedom to fixed forms. Originally the presiding clergy were free to pray in their own words, but later they were expected, and even required, to read the traditional prayers. The danger of heresy was a factor in this development.

(4) New elements usually displace older ones. In the By-

zantine divine office, the hymns tend to replace the original psalms. But the old ways sometimes survive in the great festivals. The prayer of the faithful disappeared from the Roman rite, except on Good Friday. And in the Roman divine office, hymns were admitted except during the Easter triduum and Easter week.

(5) The old liturgies were inspired by the Bible, but in a subtle way. Later use of the Bible was more explicit.[33] Also, the later liturgies were affected by the doctrinal controversies of the time. The prayers of the Roman Missal were often directed against the Pelagian heresy, even on Easter Sunday.

There can be exceptions to these laws, or retrograde movements, as Baumstark called them, but they can generally serve as a reliable guide to the evolution of the Christian year.

TWO

The Christian Roman Empire

A New Era

Christians were granted religious toleration by the so-called Edict of Milan in 313, and under the reign of the emperor Constantine their legal and financial status greatly improved. Under the circumstances we would expect to find Christian worship becoming more public and more elaborate. But according to the famous theory of Gregory Dix, the fourth century saw a more fundamental change in the liturgy, a shift from the eschatological outlook of the early Christians to the historical approach of all later eras.[1] Originally, he claimed, the Sunday eucharist was only secondarily a memorial of the resurrection. Primarily, it celebrated our eternal redemption in Christ, and looked forward to the life of the world to come. That was also true of the two annual feasts of Easter and Pentecost, also celebrated on Sunday. The early Christians knew about the life and death and resurrection of Jesus, but they were more concerned with his coming again in the near future.

In the fourth century, according to Gregory Dix, Christian worship shifted its focus from the future to the past. The saving events of the life of Christ, formerly celebrated together in the one Easter festival, were fragmented into the separate feastdays of the modern Christian calendar. The person responsible for this "liturgical revolution" was St. Cyril of Jerusalem, bishop of Jerusalem from 349 to 386. As Jerusalem became a great goal of Christian pilgrims, Cyril organized religious services at the appropriate sites, on the appropriate days, especially during Holy Week and the week of Easter. The birth of Jesus was commemorated at Bethlehem, only six miles away. Other churches copied the Jerusalem rites and accepted this "disintegration" of the liturgy into separate historical memorials.

This theory can be, has been questioned.[2] It has been pointed out that "history and eschatology are not mutually exclusive."[3] The early Christians were very much interested in the historical events of the life of Christ, and later Christians were (and are) aware that the Christ who died and rose again is also present in their midst and will come again in glory. Furthermore, the influence of Jerusalem on the liturgy, while considerable, should not be exaggerated.

The Development of Christmas

The Christmas and Epiphany feasts of the birth of Christ were observed in the fourth century, if not earlier, but the whole subject is shrouded in mystery. The Christmas feast is first mentioned in the Chronograph of the year 354, which lists the burial dates for the bishops of Rome and the burial dates for the martyrs venerated in Rome.[4] It is sometimes known as the Philocalian Calendar. The list of martyrs (the oldest liturgical calendar of the Roman church) has twenty-four entries, beginning with the "Birth of Christ in Bethlehem of Judea" on December 25. Evidently Christmas was included in the list of martyrs because it fell on a fixed date, like the feasts of the martyrs and unlike the Easter festival. Christmas was therefore being celebrated by 354 at the latest, and probably much earlier. The matching list of Roman bishops, which begins with Dionysius on December 27 and ends with Eutychian on December 8, has two additional names: Marcus, who died in 336, and Julius, who died in 352. The latest entry on the original list was Sylvester, who died on December 31, 335, which means that the calendar was compiled in 336.

An even earlier date for Christmas is suggested by a remark of St. Augustine. In one of his Epiphany sermons, he criticized the Donatists for not celebrating the Epiphany with the rest of the Catholic Church.[5] We can presume that the Donatists did celebrate Christmas, but they separated from the Catholic Church before the Epiphany was adopted in North Africa and Rome. Since the Donatist schism dates from 311, Christmas could have been established around the year 300 or earlier. If it had been introduced after the schism, the Donatists would have rejected it along with the Epiphany.

We do not know the date of Christ's birth, nor do we know the reason why December 25 was chosen for the feast of Christmas. The usual explanation is that December 25 was a pagan festival of the winter solstice, the *Natalis solis invicti* (Birthday of the Unconquered Sun), which was converted into a Christian festival. The emperor Aurelian had instituted the worship of the Unconquered Sun in A.D. 274, possibly in response to the growing popularity of the Christian God. This solar monotheism would later be adopted by the emperor Constantine, who continued to favor this sun worship even after his conversion to Christianity. His decree of 321, making Sunday a day of rest, calls it "the venerable day of the Sun," not the Christian Lord's day.[6] Obviously Constantine would have been very pleased with a feast that celebrated both the birth of Christ and the birth of the Sun, even if he was not personally involved in establishing it.

From the Christian point of view, changing the pagan feast day into a Christian one could be seen as another example of the triumph of Christianity. This would be all the easier because Christ was identified with the "sun of righteousness" in Malachi 3:20.[7] He is the true Unconquered Sun. In 243 the author (Pseudo-Cyprian) of *De pascha computus* actually associated the text from Malachi with the birth of Jesus, although he gave March 28 as the date of the nativity rather than December 25.[8] He thought that Christ died on March 25, which would also be the day of creation. Since the sun was created on the fourth day, that would be March 28, and that would also be the day when Christ, the sun of righteousness, was born. This at least indicates that in the year 243 there was still room for different opinions about the date of Christ's birth.

Even earlier Hippolytus of Rome had assigned the death of Christ to March 25, and in his *Commentary on Daniel* he supposedly gave December 25 as the day of Christ's birth.[9] But the December date is generally regarded as an interpolation.[10] Even if the text happened to be genuine, that would not mean that a feast was being celebrated on that day in the early years of the third century.

The March 25 date for the death of Christ suggests an alternative explanation for the origin of Christmas. It is quite possible that December 25 was chosen for the birth of Christ without reference to the pagan feast. Actually the theory of a pagan origin assumed that Christmas had just recently been instituted when the Philocalian Calendar was first compiled in 336. That would be after the triumph of Christianity, under the emperor Constantine and possibly at his instigation. But if Christmas dates from around the year 300, prior to the Donatist schism, the theory does not look very plausible. A victorious church might feel secure enough to appropriate a pagan feast, but the church was not yet victorious.

The alternative theory, as proposed by Louis Duchesne, begins with the belief that Christ died on March 25.[11] That happened to be the day of the official spring equinox. Actually March 25 could not have been the day of Christ's death, and of course it was not celebrated as such. The paschal feast was still determined by the lunar calendar. But if March 25 was the symbolic, if not actual, day of Christ's death, then, for reasons of symmetry, it must have been the day of his birth *or* conception. Since the latter option prevailed, the birth of Christ would come nine months later, on December 25. If that happened to be the feast of the Unconquered Sun, that was either irrelevant or, for someone like Constantine, a happy coincidence. This theory has recently been given serious consideration.[12]

The Origin of Epiphany

The theory had the additional advantage of explaining not only the origin of Christmas but also the origin of the Epiphany on January 6. In the *Church History* of Sozomen we are told that a Montanist sect celebrated the paschal feast on April 6.[13] By the same reasoning, April 6 would also be the date of the incarnation, and the birth of Christ would come nine months later, on January 6. According to Dr. Talley, April 6 was equivalent to the fourteenth day of Artemisios, the first month of spring in the Julian calendar used in Asia Minor, which differed from the calendar used in Rome.[14] He believes that this date was used by the Quartodeciman Christians in Asia, and not just by the Montanists, as Sozomen thought, as the solar equivalent of the fourteenth day of the moon in the lunar calendar.

It has often been suggested that the Epiphany, like Christmas, was originally a pagan feast, celebrated in Egypt on or about January 6. It seems that the birth of Aion was celebrated in Alexandria on January 5 and had some connection with the winter solstice. Be that as it may, the oldest reference to a Christian feast in honor of the baptism of Christ (not his birth) happens to be in the writings of Clement of Alexandria.[15] It was celebrated, not by the orthodox Christians, but by the followers of Basilides (a Gnostic sect). Some kept the feast on the fifteenth of Tybi (January 10), and others on the eleventh (January 6). This comment comes in the midst of a chronology linking the birth and death of Christ with the reigns of the Roman emperors.

The Epiphany, or "manifestation," of Christ could refer to his birth as well as his baptism, and of course it was possible to think of both events as occurring on the same day, thirty years apart (Lk 3:23). The emphasis on the baptism in Alexandria may have something to do with the theology of the Gnostics, or it may serve as an example of the influence of the gospel of Mark in the church of Egypt. That gospel begins, not with the birth of Jesus, but with his baptism. As the other eastern churches adopted the feast, the emphasis shifted to the birth of Christ, but in most cases the baptism-theme was not forgotten. It would later be restored when those churches accepted the Roman feast of Christmas on December 25.

At Constantinople the Christmas feast was celebrated at least from the accession of the emperor Theodosius I in 379, who restored orthodoxy after a series of emperors who favored Arianism. It was also celebrated at Antioch, but it was not introduced at Alexandria until the fifth century, and it seems that Jerusalem resisted even longer. At least by the sixth century, all the eastern churches except the Armenian celebrated the birth of Christ at Christmas and his baptism on the Epiphany. To this day the Armenian church has no Christmas feast, except in those churches in union with Rome.

In the west, meanwhile, the Epiphany was added to the Christmas feast. In Gaul the Epiphany was probably introduced even before Christmas, but it was not unusual for eastern influences to reach Gaul directly, without affecting the Roman church. In Rome it was not included in the list of feasts in the Chronograph of 354, when Liberius was bishop, but may have been added under his successor, Damasus (366–384). That would be about the same time that the feast of Christmas was being imported to the east. The western churches, however, kept the Epiphany as a second Christmas feast, with the adoration of the magi as the principal theme. In Gaul (and eventually in Rome), the baptism of the Lord and the miracle at Cana were included in the *tria miracula* of the Epiphany, but they were barely mentioned in the liturgy. When the Epiphany was given an octave in the eighth century, the gospel reading for the octave day on January 13 was the Lord's baptism. The miracle at Cana was the gospel reading for the second Sunday after Epiphany. In the Byzantine rite, on the other hand, the adoration of the magi is the gospel reading for Christmas day, and so it is not treated as a theme distinct from the nativity itself.

Holy Week in Jerusalem

The late fourth century also saw a considerable development of the Easter liturgy. For the Easter services in Jerusalem we have the very valuable descriptions in the travel diary of a pilgrim from the west (perhaps from Spain or Gaul), a nun who visited the holy places between 381 and 384. There is some uncertainty about her name, but she is usually known as Egeria.[16] Jerusalem, renamed Aelia Capitolina, had been rebuilt as a pagan city by the emperor Hadrian after the second Jewish revolt (132–135), and more recently had become the goal of Christian pilgrims to the holy places. The site of the Jewish temple was still in ruins at the time of her visit, but she often mentions the church on Sion, at the place where the disciples of Jesus had gathered together on the day of Pentecost. It would also be identified as the upper room where the last supper took place.

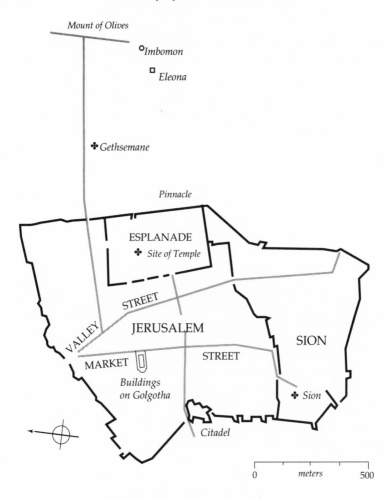

Mount of Olives

○ *Imbomon*

□ *Eleona*

♣ *Gethsemane*

Pinnacle

ESPLANADE
♣ *Site of Temple*

STREET

VALLEY

JERUSALEM

SION

MARKET   STREET

*Buildings
on Golgotha*

♣ *Sion*

Citadel

0   *meters*   500

FOURTH-CENTURY JERUSALEM

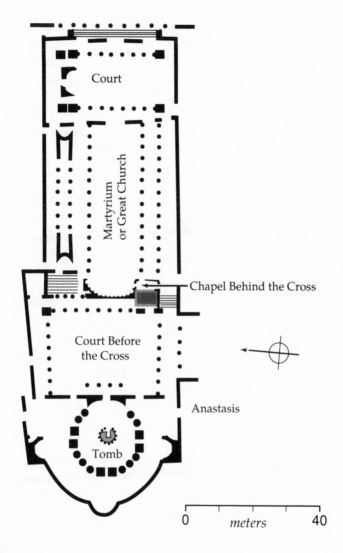

Court

Martyrium or Great Church

Chapel Behind the Cross

Court Before the Cross

Anastasis

Tomb

0   *meters*   40

CONSTANTINE'S BUILDINGS ON GOLGOTHA
IN THE TIME OF EGERIA

Although the Sion church was still important, most of the religious services described by Egeria now took place at the tomb of Christ and the nearby site of the crucifixion. This was one of the many churches built by the emperor Constantine, and was described by Eusebius in his *Life of Constantine.*[17] The basilica, known as the Martyrium, was on the east side of the holy sepulcher, with a courtyard between the two buildings. The site of the crucifixion was marked by a chapel in the southeast corner of the courtyard. The holy sepulcher, as Egeria described it, was enclosed by a circular structure known as the Anastasis, or Resurrection. As in other Constantinian churches (e.g. St. Peter's in Rome), the main entrance to the basilica was at the east end and the altar was at the west end, contrary to the normal orientation.[18]

There was also a church on the Mount of Olives, known as the Eleona, over the cave where Christ instructed his disciples before his ascension, and a church of the Holy Ascension was built nearby, probably after Egeria's visit, at the place she called the Imbomon. At Bethany there was a church at the tomb of Lazarus, and at Bethlehem Constantine had built the church of the Nativity over the cave where Christ was born.

In Egeria's time, the fast before Easter had been extended from one or two days to the forty days of Lent. In the west every day of Lent was a fast day, except the Sundays. In the east there was no fasting on Saturdays and Sundays, except on Holy Saturday. Since there were only five fast days each week, the Lenten season began eight weeks before Easter. During Lent the usual daily offices were celebrated: morning and evening prayer, and a short office at noon and three o'clock, with an additional office at nine in the morning. During the rest of the year there was no service at nine o'clock. The offices were usually celebrated in the Anastasis, and the eucharist in the Martyrium, also known as the Great Church.

During Holy Week in Jerusalem, there were so many

extra services at so many different places that the people were totally exhausted, as Egeria admits. It began on the day before Palm Sunday, the day still observed as Lazarus Saturday in the Greek church. On Saturday afternoon the people went to the Lazarium at Bethany. The service included the reading of John 12:1, "Six days before Passover Jesus came to Bethany, where Lazarus was, whom Jesus had raised from the dead." (In the Roman rite, this pericope is read on Monday in Holy Week, six days before the *Christian* Passover, or Easter.) On Palm Sunday mass was celebrated as usual in the morning, in the Great Church, but in the afternoon the people went to the Eleona church on the Mount of Olives, and then to the Imbomon at the summit, where the gospel was read about Christ's entry into Jerusalem from the Mount of Olives. Then they returned to the city carrying palm branches, and stayed for a late vespers at the Anastasis.

On the next three days of Holy Week there were the usual services, but the afternoon service at three o'clock was prolonged until seven in the evening, followed immediately by evening prayer. On Tuesday night, "late though it is," they went to the Eleona church on the Mount of Olives, where the bishop reads the discourse that Jesus gave there (Mt 24 and 25). On Wednesday night, after the usual visit to the Anastasis, the people remain in the church for the reading of the next chapter (Mt 26:3–16), about Judas agreeing to betray Jesus. These readings are still used today in the Greek liturgy. In the Roman rite, before Vatican II, the passion according to Mark was read on Tuesday, and the passion according to Luke on Wednesday. These were replaced by the accounts of the betrayal of Jesus in John 13:21–38 on Tuesday and in Matthew 26:14–25 on Wednesday. The gospel for Wednesday also serves as the beginning of the passion according to Matthew read on Palm Sunday.

On Holy Thursday there were the usual services in the

morning and at noon, but the three o'clock service was held an hour early in the Great Church, followed by the eucharist. A second mass was celebrated immediately after in the chapel of the Crucifixion, the only day of the year when a mass was celebrated there. After the usual visit to the Anastasis, there was just time for a quick meal before going to the Mount of Olives for an all-night vigil. At the Eleona church the vigil service included the reading of the last supper discourses in John 13:16–18:1. Around midnight they went up to the Imbomon, and at cockcrow they descended to a church built "where the Lord prayed," and heard the gospel reading about the agony in the garden and the arrest of Jesus (Mt 26:31–56). From Gethsemane they returned to the city around sunrise, and there they were told about the encounter between Jesus and Pontius Pilate (Jn 18:28–19:16). Then the bishop, after some words of encouragement, allowed them to go home for a short rest until the next service at eight o'clock.

It was now Good Friday, and the first service of the day was the veneration of the cross. The relic, held by the bishop and guarded by deacons, was placed on a table in the chapel of the Crucifixion and was kissed by the people as they passed through the chapel. In the afternoon, from noon until three o'clock, there was a liturgical service in the courtyard, ending with the gospel reading about the death of Christ on the cross (Jn 19:17–37). The people then moved into the Great Church for the three o'clock service, which, as usual during Holy Week, was prolonged until seven o'clock and ended with evening prayer. Finally, they went to the Anastasis for the gospel reading about the burial of Christ (Mt 27:57–61). They were now free to retire for the night, although some stayed on to spend the night in prayer.

On Holy Saturday the eucharist was not celebrated, as it normally would be on Saturdays. There was the usual Lenten office at nine in the morning, and the office at noon, but nothing else until the Easter vigil began in the evening. Egeria did not bother to describe the liturgy of the Easter vigil because it was the same as the liturgy she was familiar with in the west. The only difference she noticed was that the bishop, right after the baptisms, brought the newly-baptized into the Anastasis for a prayer before bringing them into the Great Church for the Easter mass (probably around midnight). A second mass was celebrated immediately afterward in the Anastasis. Presumably the second mass, on this and other occasions, was celebrated without a liturgy of the word. Egeria mentions that they do not waste any time during the vigil, so that the people can be dismissed as soon as possible.

The Easter Vigil

Although Egeria did not describe the Jerusalem Easter vigil, a lectionary for the services in Jerusalem in the fifth century was discovered in an Armenian manuscript based on a Greek original.[19] According to the lectionary there were twelve Bible readings at the vigil service in the Great Church. The readings were as follows:

1. The creation story (Gen 1:1–3:24)
2. The testing of Abraham (Gen 22:1–18)
3. The Passover ritual prescribed (Ex 12:1–24)
4. The story of Jonah (Jon 1:1–4:11)
5. The crossing of the Red Sea (Ex 14:24–15:21)
6. The glory of the new Zion (Is 60:1–13)
7. The Lord's answer to Job (Job 38:1–28)
8. The ascension of Elijah (2 Kgs 2:1–22)
9. The new covenant (Jer 31:31–34)
10. The promised land (Jos 1:1–9)
11. The valley of dry bones (Ez 37:1–14)
12. The story of the three young men (Dan 3:1–90 in LXX version).[20]

The first three of those readings show the continuity between the Jewish Passover and the Christian Pascha.[21] The last reading was followed by the epistle (1 Cor 15:1-11) and gospel (Mt 28:1-20) of the Easter mass. Later, at the Anastasis, the resurrection gospel from John was read before the second mass.

Down through the centuries there was some variety in the choice and number of readings for the Easter vigil in the various Christian churches. Before 1951 the Roman Missal had twelve lessons (an asterisk indicates agreement with the Jerusalem list):

1. *The creation story (Gen 1:1-2:2)
2. Noah and the great flood (Gen 5:32-8:21)
3. *The testing of Abraham (Gen 22:1-19)
4. *The crossing of the Red Sea (Ex 14:24-15:1)
5. Israel's restoration (Is 54:17-55:11)
6. Wisdom leads to life (Bar 3:9-38)
7. *The valley of dry bones (Ez 37:1-14)
8. Jerusalem's restoration (Is 4:1-6)
9. *The Passover ritual prescribed (Ex 12:1-11)
10. *The story of Jonah (Jon 3:1-10)
11. The testament of Moses (Dt 31:22-30)
12. *The story of the three young men (Dan 3:1-24).

The first and last readings in both lists are the same. The first five and the last two readings in the Jerusalem list also appear in the Roman list. The reform of the Roman Easter vigil in 1951 resulted in a reduction of the number of lessons to four, namely, lessons one, four, eight and eleven (the Gregorian Sacramentary only had four lessons). But the Roman Missal of 1970 provided seven lessons, *ad libitum,* with directions to read at least three of them, and never to omit the reading of Exodus 14. They are as follows:

1. The creation story (Gen 1:1-2:2)
2. The testing of Abraham (Gen 22:1-18)

3. The crossing of the Red Sea (Ex 14:15–15:1)
4. Israel restored (Is 54:5–14)
5. Israel restored (Is 55:1–11)
6. Wisdom leads to life (Bar 3:9–15, 32–37; 4:1–4)
7. A new heart and a new spirit (Ez 36:16–28)

Only the first three of these lessons were read in the Jerusalem vigil service. They were also in the old Roman list, along with lessons five and six (with some rearrangement of the verses). The Passover regulations (Ex 12) were formerly read twice in the Roman rite, as the second lesson on Good Friday and the ninth lesson of the Easter vigil, but the reading has now been transferred to the Mass of the Lord's Supper on Holy Thursday.

In the Byzantine rite the vigil service has fifteen lessons from the Old Testament. They include eight of the readings from the Jerusalem list, namely, lessons one to six, and lessons nine and twelve. The epistle of the vigil mass is Romans 6:3–11 and the gospel is Matthew 28:1–20. The gospel, but not the epistle, is the same as in the Jerusalem rite and (in a shorter form) the Roman rite.

The Easter Festival

According to Egeria, the Easter festival was celebrated in Jerusalem for eight days, "as people do everywhere else." Apparently another mass was celebrated on Easter morning. The epistle, in the Armenian Lectionary, was Acts 1:1–14, and the gospel was Mark 15:42–16:8. In the Byzantine rite this is the mass said at midnight, since the vigil mass is now said earlier. The readings are from Acts 1:1–9 and John 1:1–17. In the Roman rite (before 1970), the readings were from 1 Corinthians 5:7–8 and Mark 16:1–7. There are now three readings: from Acts 10:34, 37–43, 1 Corinthians 5:6–8 (or Colossians

3:1–4), and John 20:1–9. The resurrection gospels of Matthew, Mark and Luke are now read at the vigil mass in a three-year cycle.

During Easter week in Jerusalem the eucharist was celebrated every day, and then the bishop brought the newly-baptized into the Anastasis for instructions in the Christian mysteries. In the afternoon they went to the Mount of Olives for special services and then returned to the Anastasis for evening prayer. On Easter Sunday and on the following Sunday there was an additional service at the Sion church, where the gospel was read about the appearances of the risen Christ in that very place (Jn 20:19–25, 26–31). On Wednesday, however, the eucharist was celebrated at the Eleona church and on Friday at the Sion church.

Egeria mentions a festival celebrated forty days after Easter, not in Jerusalem but in the church of the Nativity in Bethlehem. The date, of course, suggests the feast of the Ascension, which was making its appearance at about that time, but strangely enough she only says that the sermons preached by the bishop and his clergy were "suitable to the place and the day." It is possible that in Jerusalem the feast had not yet been introduced; it would later be celebrated at the Imbomon on the Mount of Olives. According to one theory, the festival in Bethlehem was actually in honor of the holy innocents.[22]

Finally, the Easter season ended on Pentecost Sunday with another exhausting round of services. After morning prayer the eucharist was celebrated in the Great Church, and then the people went to the Sion church for a second mass at nine o'clock, at the very time when the disciples received the Holy Spirit, and in the very place. After a break for lunch, they went to the Imbomon on the Mount of Olives, where the gospel of the Ascension was read, and then to the Eleona for evening prayer. Returning to the city in a slow procession,

they arrived at the Great Church around eight o'clock for
services there and in the Anastasis. Then they returned to the
Sion church, and were finally dismissed around midnight. As
Egeria observed, it was "a very hard day for them."

Other Jerusalem Feasts

In addition to Easter and its octave, two other feasts were
celebrated in Jerusalem with an octave: the Epiphany and the
Dedication feast. The Epiphany was still the only feast of the
birth of Christ, since they had not yet adopted Christmas. It
began with a vigil service in Bethlehem on January 5, with a
midnight mass. The bishop then returned to Jerusalem for a
morning mass in the Great Church. During the octave the
eucharist was celebrated there on the first three days, and then
at other churches on the following days. On February 14 the
"fortieth day" was celebrated in the Anastasis as a major feast
day. It would later be known as Hypapante or Meeting, that is,
the meeting of Christ and Simeon in the temple (Lk 2:22–38).
When Christmas replaced Epiphany as the day of the nativity,
Hypapante was moved to February 2. In the west it was originally known by its Greek name, and later as the Purification
of the Blessed Virgin Mary. Since 1970 it has been retitled the
Presentation of the Lord and is no longer classified as a Marian feast.

The dedication of the Great Church in Jerusalem was
also celebrated with an octave. Egeria compared it to the dedication of the temple by Solomon, and there was the more
recent dedication (Hanukkah in Hebrew, Encaenia in Greek)
by the Maccabees (1 Mac 4:59; 2 Mac 10:5–6). The date was
September 13, still observed in the Byzantine rite. On the
same day, it was said, they discovered the cross of Christ, and
so the Exaltation of the Holy Cross was celebrated on Sep-

tember 14. This feast (but not the dedication) was later adopted in the west. In the Byzantine rite, the octave has been transferred to the feast of the Holy Cross.

The last section of Egeria's diary is missing; it probably contained a description of the local saints' days. These can be found, for a somewhat later period, in the Armenian lectionary. Several of them were Old Testament prophets who are still honored in the Byzantine rite but not in the west. They included Jeremiah (May 1), Zechariah (June 10), Elisha (June 14), Isaiah (July 6), and "James and David" (December 25). James, i.e. Jacob, may have been the patriarch originally, but was later venerated as James the Lord's brother, the first bishop of Jerusalem. The memorial was displaced by Christmas, and now appears in the Greek calendar on the Sunday after Christmas. The Maccabees (August 1) were the only Old Testament martyrs commemorated in all the churches, east and west, but were removed from the Roman calendar in 1969.[23] The story of the martyrs is found in 2 Maccabees 6 and 7.

The saints of the New Testament in the Jerusalem calendar included John the Baptist (August 29), Mary the Mother of God (August 15), the Holy Innocents (May 9 or 18), the Apostle Thomas and Others (August 23 or 24), the Apostle Philip (November 15), the Apostle Andrew (November 30), St. Stephen (December 27), the Apostles Paul and Peter (December 28), the Apostle James and Evangelist John (December 29). The last three memorials were apparently assigned to the octave of Christmas, and were added to the Jerusalem calendar despite the fact that Christmas was not celebrated there. They were mentioned as customary feast days by St. Gregory of Nyssa in 379.[24] The Armenian church, which still has a memorial of David and James the Lord's brother on December 25 instead of Christmas, has retained these three feasts, but one day earlier.

Finally, the Jerusalem calendar also listed a few of the later Christian saints. Eusebius of Caesarea, in his *Martyrs of Palestine,* knew of eighty-three local martyrs put to death during the years 303 to 311, but only one of them appears in the calendar, and they managed to get his name wrong: Peter Abshelama is listed as Peter and Abisalom (January 11). The others are St. Antony of Egypt (January 17), Emperor Theodosius (January 19), the Forty Martyrs of Sebaste (March 9), St. Cyril of Jerusalem (March 18), St. John of Jerusalem (March 29), and Emperor Constantine (May 22). Also, the Apparition of the Cross over Jerusalem in 351 (May 7), described by Cyril in a letter to Constantius.[25] The event is still commemorated in the Byzantine calendar.

The Roman Martyrs

For the saints venerated in Rome, we have the Chronograph of 354, which is also the oldest evidence for the Christmas feast on December 25. There are twenty-four entries, and they illustrate very nicely the primitive rules for honoring the saints. They are all martyrs, and almost all of them are local martyrs. They are local, not just in the sense that they are Romans, but in the stricter sense that the location of the tomb is given along with the name and date of death. In most cases the year of death is not given and was probably not known; they had to know the anniversary day, but it was not necessary to know the year.

Two of the entries in the calendar were for non-Roman martyrs, both of them African (the Roman and African churches had very close ties). They were for Perpetua and Felicity (March 7) and Cyprian of Carthage (September 14). Cyprian's name is followed by a note that in Rome his feast is celebrated in the cemetery of Callistus. There were no entries for biblical saints, not even for St. John the Baptist or the Virgin Mary, except for the apostles Peter and Paul, who were honored because they were *Roman* martyrs.

The apostles Peter and Paul have a common feast on June 29, which presents a number of problems. It is generally assumed that they died in different years, and therefore on different days. If June 29 was not their day of death or burial, it could be the date of some other event, such as the translation of their relics. And in fact Peter is located at the catacombs, not at the Vatican, while Paul is located on the Via Ostia. Also, the year is given: in the consulship of Tuscus and Bassus, which would be A.D. 258 if the entry is correct. What happened in the year 258, and why is the cult of St. Peter connected with the catacombs (the church of St. Sebastian) on the Via Appia? There have been many attempts to answer these questions, but the mystery remains.[26] In any case, the Roman date for the feast of Sts. Peter and Paul prevailed over the eastern tradition of assigning them to Christmas week (except in the Armenian church).

The calendar also has a feast of St. Peter's Chair (Natale Petri de Cathedra) on February 22. The date is usually explained as a Christian substitute for the pagan commemoration of deceased family members at the end of the year (February was originally the last month), when a chair was left empty at the memorial banquet.[27] Later generations would think of it as the beginning of Peter's apostleship, since it was customary to celebrate the day of a bishop's installation.[28] When the feast was adopted in Gaul it was usually transferred to January 18 to avoid conflict with the Lenten season. The two dates for the feast were sometimes explained by assigning Peter's Chair at Rome to the January date and his Chair at Antioch to the February date. The two feasts were finally added to the Roman calendar in 1558, but in 1960 the January feast was abolished and the original title was restored to the feast on February 22.

The other Roman martyrs seem to belong to a much later period, the third century or the persecution of Diocletian in the early fourth century. The oldest entry is for Pope Callistus, who died in 222. This is the list of saints, with the dates changed to the modern equivalents:[29]

Dec. 25   Natus Christus in Betleem Iudeae.

Jan. 20   Fabiani in Callisti et Sebastiani in Catacumbas.

Jan. 21   Agnetis in Nomentana.

Feb. 22   Natale Petri de cathedra.

Mar. 7   Perpetuae et Felicitatis, Africae.

May 19   Partheni et Caloceri in Callisti (A.D. 304).

June 29   Petri in Catacumbas et Pauli Ostense (A.D. 258).

July 10   Felicis et Filippi in Priscillae; et in Iordanorum Martialis, Vitalis, Alexandri; et in Maximi Silani, hunc Silanum martirem Novati furati sunt; et in Pretextatae, Ianuari.

July 30   Abdos et Sennes in Pontiani, quod est ad Ursum piliatum.

Aug. 6   Xysti in Callisti; et in Praetextati, Agapiti et Felicissimi.

Aug. 8   Secundi, Carpofori, Victorini et Severiani in Albano; et Ostense VII ballistaria, Cyriaci, Largi, Crescentiani, Memmiae, Iulianae et Smaragdi.

Aug. 9   Laurenti in Tiburtina.

Aug. 13   Ypoliti in Tiburtina et Pontiani in Callisti.

Aug. 22   Timotei, Ostense.

Aug. 28   Hermetis in Basillae Salaria vetere.

Sep. 5   Aconti in Porto, et Nonni et Herculani et Taurini.

Sep. 9   Gorgoni in Labicana.

Sep. 11   Proti et Iacinti, in Basillae.

Sep. 14   Cypriani, Africae, Romae celebratur in Callisti.

Sep. 22   Basillae, Salaria vetere (A.D. 304).

Oct. 14   Callisti in Via Aurelia, miliario III.

Nov. 9   Clementis, Semproniani, Claudi, Nicostrati in comitatum.

Nov. 29   Saturnini in Trasonis.

Dec. 13   Ariston in Portum.

All but five of these entries (May 19, September 5, September 22, November 9, December 13) could still be found in the Roman calendar in 1969. In that year there was a drastic reduction in the number of feast days, affecting nine of the remaining entries. They are now limited to a local cult, i.e. in the churches dedicated to their memory in Rome or elsewhere. The reason for their removal was that nothing was known about them except their names and dates.

The Christian cemeteries, with their catacombs, can be found along all the roads leading out of Rome. Pope Damasus (366–384) provided suitable inscriptions for the tombs of the martyrs buried there. But they were gradually abandoned during the dark ages because of the barbarian invasions.[30] Many of the bodies of the saints were transferred to churches in the city. The catacombs were rediscovered in the sixteenth century, and excavations have been carried out ever since.

On the Via Aurelia, west of the city, is the cemetery of Calepodius, where Pope Callistus (October 14) was buried. On the Via Ostia, to the south, are the tombs of St. Paul (June 29) and St. Timothy (August 22). On the Via Appia, also to the south, are the cemeteries of Callistus, Praetextatus and

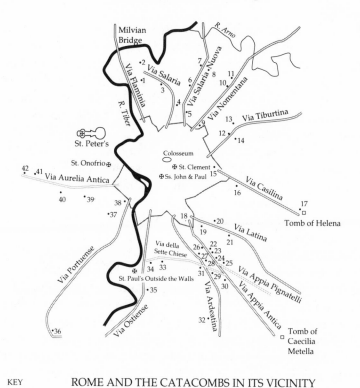

KEY

ROME AND THE CATACOMBS IN ITS VICINITY

1 Valentine

2 'Ad Clivum Cucumeris' [?]

3 Bassilla (Hermes)

4 Pamphilus

5 Felicity

6 Thrason

7 Priscilla

8 Jordani

9 Nicomedes

10 Agnes

11 Coemeterium Maius

12 Novatian

13 Hippolytus

14 Cyriaca (St. Lawrence)

15 Hypogaeum of the Aurelii

16 Castulus

17 Peter and Marcellinus

18 Campana

19 Gordian and Epimachus

20 Apronian

21 Via Dino Campagni (Via Latina)

22 Vibia

23 The Hunters

24 The Cross (Sta Croce)

25 Praetextatus

26 Soter

27 Balbina

28 Basileus (Marcus and Marcellianus)

29 Callistus (incl. Lucina)

30 'Ad Catacumbas' (St Sebastian)

31 Domitilla

32 Nunziatella

33 Commodilla

34 Timothy

35 Thecla

36 Generosa

37 Pontian

38 'Ad Insalsatos' [?]

39 Pancras

40 Processus and Martinian

41 'Duo Felices'

42 Calepodius

"Ad catacumbas" under the church of St. Sebastian, where many popes and martyrs were buried. On the Via Labicana, to the east, in the cemetery "Ad duas lauros," are the tombs of St. Tiburtius and Sts. Peter and Marcellinus, and also St. Gorgonius (September 9). On the Via Tiburtina, also to the east, is the cemetery of St. Hippolytus (August 13), and on the Via Nomentana, to the north, there are several cemeteries, notably that of St. Agnes (January 21). Also north of the city are the cemeteries on the Via Salaria Nova and the Via Salaria Vetus, where St. Basilla (September 22), St. Hermes (August 28), and Sts. Protus and Hyacinth (September 11) were buried. On the Via Flaminia, to the north, is the cemetery of St. Valentine. Finally, returning to the west, there is the tomb of St. Peter on the Vatican.

These were only a few of the saints whose tombs were venerated in the cemeteries surrounding the city. Pilgrims could obtain guide books to take with them as they circled clockwise or counter-clockwise; the books were in use from the seventh century. Later, of course, the saints were translated to the various city churches, which made things easier for the church authorities. In the old days, for example, services for the Seven Brothers (July 10) were held in three different places, since two of them were in the cemetery of Priscilla and three more in the Jordani cemetery, and the others were in the cemeteries of Maximus and Praetextatus (the first two cemeteries adjoined one another, and had a combined service).[31]

Apparently the first translation from a cemetery to a Roman church took place in 648, when Pope Theodore I brought the relics of Sts. Primus and Felician to the church of St. Stephen (Santo Stefano Rotondo). Their tomb on the Via Nomentana was fourteen miles away, too far to be easily visited. But the rest of the church was not as conservative as Rome. The translation of relics in other churches, especially in the east, had been going on since the fourth century. The earliest recorded translation was that of St. Babylas of Antioch, who was martyred around the year 250. In 351 his remains were moved to a church at Daphne, a few miles away, which caused the nearby oracle of Apollo to fall silent. But in 362 the emperor Julian the Apostate ordered the relics to be returned to Antioch.

In 386 St. Ambrose was about to dedicate a new church in Milan, later known as the Ambrosian Basilica, when he was inspired to discover the remains of the martyrs Gervasius and Protasius, buried in the cemetery church of Sts. Nabor and Felix. Miraculous cures took place, and the bodies were enshrined in the new basilica, where Ambrose himself was later buried.[32] They were rediscovered in 1864. Another inspired discovery took place in 395, when Ambrose found the bodies of Sts. Nazarius and Celsus in a garden outside the city and brought them to the Basilica of the Apostles.[33] He also had the body of his predecessor, St. Dionysius, returned from Cappadocia, where he had died in exile. It was sent by St. Basil, along with a letter certifying that this was really Dionysius.[34] All this was going on despite laws forbidding the translation of relics and the dismemberment and sale of the bodies of the martyrs.[35]

Meanwhile the feasts of the more popular saints were being celebrated throughout the Christian world; they were no longer limited to a memorial service at the tomb. Even the Roman church admitted some of these festivals to their local calendar, but if they didn't have the body, they usually had a church or chapel dedicated to the saint. In that way the saint became Roman by adoption, as it were. Thus Sts. Gervasius and Protasius of Milan had a church in Rome, the *titulus* Vestinae, later dedicated to St. Vitalis, who was supposedly the father of the two martyrs. The very popular Sts. Cosmas and Damian, who were buried at Cyrrhus in Syria, were given a chapel in St. Mary Major's, and later Pope Felix IV (526–530) remodeled two pagan temples in the Forum and joined them to serve as a church for the saints. The church of St. Theodore, built around the same time, honored the memory of the soldier-saint buried at Euchaita in Pontus, and replaced an even older church with that name.

Saints But Not Martyrs

Another change affecting the calendar was the acceptance of saints who were not martyrs. Originally the anniversaries of the local bishops were listed separately from the anniversaries of the local martyrs, but their memorial services would have been similar if not identical. In Rome they eventually solved the problem by honoring *all* the early bishops as martyrs, including Pope Sylvester, who was elected in 314, after the persecutions had ended. St. Martin of Tours, the most famous of the "confessors" (non-martyrs), died in 397. A hundred years later Pope Symmachus built a chapel in his honor at the *titulus* Equitii, later known as the church of St. Sylvester, and still later as the church of St. Martin. But it seems that there was some delay in adding his name to the Roman calendar.[36] And another St. Martin, this one a martyr, was associated with the church. Pope Martin I died in exile in 656 and was buried in the Crimea. His relics were supposedly returned to Rome and enshrined in the church of St. Martin, and his feast day was assigned to November 12, the day after the feast of St. Martin of Tours (it was moved to April 13 in 1969).

Despite the admission of saints who were not martyrs, to this day the Byzantine calendar is still mainly a list of martyrs. That was also true of the Roman calendar during the middle ages and at the time of the Tridentine reform in the sixteenth century. Since then, however, most of the saints added to the calendar were not martyrs, and many of the ancient martyrs were removed after Vatican II.

There were no biblical saints in the Roman calendar of 354, except for Sts. Peter and Paul, and not many were added before the middle ages. St. John the Baptist had two festivals: his birth on June 24 and his death on August 29. His birthday obviously depended on the feast of Christmas, and shared the same western origin. According to Luke 1:26, John was conceived, and therefore born, six months before Jesus. In the Roman reckoning, that would be June 24, not June 25, because June 24 was the eighth day before the Kalends of July, corresponding to Christmas on the eighth day before the Kalends of January. It was the time of the summer solstice, opposite Christmas at the winter solstice, which symbolized the relationship between John and Jesus: "He must increase; I must decrease" (Jn 3:30). The days get shorter after John's birthday, and they get longer after Christmas. And since Jesus said of John: "I tell you, among those born of women, no one is greater than John" (Lk 7:28), his feast became a major holy day in the west and also in the east.

The feast of the Beheading (Decollation) of John the Baptist on August 29 was borrowed from the church of Jerusalem, and was probably the dedication day of his church in Samaria, the traditional site of his tomb. The Greek church added several additional feasts not found in the Roman rite: a commemoration on January 7 (because of his role in the baptism of Christ on January 6), the First and Second Finding of his head on February 24, the Third Finding of his head on May 25, and his Conception on September 23. Many churches claimed to have John's head, including the church of St. Sylvester (San Silvestro in Capite), the English church in Rome. Pope Hilary (461–468) added chapels dedicated to John the Baptist and John the Evangelist to the baptistry of the Lateran Basilica, later known as St. John Lateran.

The saints of Christmas week are missing from the Roman calendar of 354, but they were soon being venerated in all the churches, along with John the Baptist. St. Stephen the First Martyr was usually assigned to December 26, but the Greek church later added a commemoration of the Mother of God on that day and moved St. Stephen to December 27. In 415 the priest Lucian claimed to have discovered the body of St. Stephen at a site north of Jerusalem. His remains were transferred to the Sion church, and then to a basilica built in his honor near the Damascus Gate (the present church was built in 1900 on the ruins of the original basilica). Portions of his relics were distributed very widely, e.g. to Constantinople, to North Africa, and to Rome, where they were deposited in the church of St. Lawrence Outside the Walls. Pope Pelagius I (556–561) had the relics of the two deacons, Stephen and Lawrence, enshrined together in the crypt.

The Greek church added a feast of the Translation of St. Stephen on August 2. In Rome that date was the anniversary of the death of Pope Stephen I (254–257), a feast removed from the general calendar in 1969. The Finding (*Inventio*) of St. Stephen was celebrated on August 3, but was removed from the general calendar in 1960.

On the days following St. Stephen's Day, the churches of the east commemorated the apostles Peter and Paul, and James and John. They were the most important of the twelve. But the Roman feast of Sts. Peter and Paul on June 29 generally prevailed over the eastern date. Only St. John was accepted in Rome, on December 27 (his brother St. James was later commemorated on July 25). Rome later added an additional feast, St. John Before the Latin Gate, on May 6 (removed from the general calendar in 1960). The story, mentioned by Tertullian around the year 200, was that John was plunged into boiling oil at the Latin Gate in Rome, but was unharmed.[37] There is still a church at the site.

The Greek church also assigned separate days for the brothers James and John. St. John has two feasts, on May 8 and his Dormition (death) on September 26. The feast of St. James is on April 30.

The feast of the Holy Innocents was commemorated in Bethlehem on May 9 or 18, according to the Armenian Lectionary, and so their feast on December 28 may be of western origin (it is on December 29 in the Byzantine calendar). Under Gallican influence, it was observed as a penitential day, with purple vestments, except when it fell on a Sunday, but it was restored as a regular martyrs' day in 1960. The three feasts of St. Stephen, St. John and the Holy Innocents were formerly celebrated even when they happened to fall on a Sunday, but they are now replaced by the feast of the Holy Family, which was assigned to the Sunday after Christmas in 1969.

The anniversary of Pope Sylvester I (314–335) on December 31 was noted in the *Depositio episcoporum* of 354. He was buried in the cemetery of Priscilla on the Via Salaria, but in 761 his relics were transferred to the church of St. Sylvester *in Capite,* now the English church in Rome. His name was originally associated with the *titulus* Equitii, later known as the church of St. Martin.

The octave of Christmas is the designation for January 1 that has persisted in the Roman rite, along with various additional titles, down to the present. As it happened to be the Roman New Year's Day, the church showed its disapproval of pagan orgies by saying the mass "against idolatry" on that day. The penitential rite was later replaced by a more festive liturgy, suitable for the octave of Christmas and with special emphasis on Mary, the Mother of God. In the medieval period it became the feast of the Circumcision and St. Martina and St. Basil.

In the Byzantine rite January 1 has always been celebrated as the feast of the Circumcision, which took place eight days after the birth of Jesus (Lk 2:21). It is also the feast of St. Basil the Great, who died on January 1, 379 at Caesarea in Cappadocia. In the west the churches of the Gallican rite adopted the feast of the Circumcision in the sixth century.

A feast of St. Michael the Archangel was celebrated in the east and in the west, originally at a church built in his honor. In the east St. Michael was invoked as patron of the sick at various springs, especially in Phrygia. His principal feast, on November 8, was associated with the Baths of Arcadius in Constantinople. An additional feast, the Miracle at Colossae (September 6), concerned a sacred spring protected by St. Michael. His principal feast in Rome, on September 29, marked the dedication of a church in his honor on the Via Salaria (no longer extant). An additional feast, the Apparition at Monte Gargano (May 8), was removed from the general calendar in 1960, but is still celebrated at the sanctuary near Manfredonia, now known as Monte Sant'Angelo.

Only two feasts of apostles were added to the Roman calendar before the ninth century: St. Andrew and Sts. Philip and James. They both date from the sixth century. St. Andrew, the brother of St. Peter, is commemorated on November 30 in the eastern and western churches—an unusual agreement. According to the Greek tradition, he was martyred at Patras in Greece, and in the fourth century his relics were brought to Constantinople, where he was honored as patron saint. When the city fell to the crusaders in 1204 the relics were taken to Amalfi in Italy. The head, however, was transferred to St. Peter's in Rome; in 1964 Pope Paul VI returned it to Patras. St. Andrew was also adopted as the patron saint of Russia (which claimed to be the successor of the Byzantine empire) and Scotland (which claimed to have some of his relics at Saint Andrews).

The feast of Sts. Philip and James on May 1 was the dedication day of the church of the Holy Apostles in Rome, built under Pelagius I (556–561) and John III (561–574). Their relics are believed to be in the crypt. This St. James is the son of Alphaeus, usually known as James the Less. The Roman tradition identifies him with James the Lord's brother, but the Greek tradition does not. The Greek church assigns separate feast days for St. Philip (November 14), St. James the Less (October 9), and St. James the Lord's brother and first bishop of Jerusalem (October 23). In 1955 the Roman feast was moved to May 11, the first free day, to make room for the feast of St. Joseph the Worker on May 1, which is observed as Labor Day in most countries. In 1969 it was moved again, to May 3.

Besides these biblical saints, a few non-Roman martyrs were added to the Roman calendar about the same time. St. Vincent, the Spanish deacon and martyr, was honored on January 22. Apparently there was no church dedicated to his memory, but his name was later attached to the monastery at Tre Fontane along with St. Anastasius, a Persian martyr whose relics were brought to the monastery church. There is also a medieval church of Sts. Vincent and Anastasius near the Trevi Fountain.

The two martyrs of Sicily, Sts. Agatha and Lucy, were added to the Roman and Byzantine calendars, St. Agatha on February 5 and St. Lucy on December 13. St. Agatha died at Catania, where her protection is sought against the eruptions of Mount Etna. In Rome the church of St. Agatha (Sant'Agata dei Goti) was used for Arian worship during the period of Gothic rule in the sixth century. St. Lucy died at Syracuse, but her relics were taken away. According to one tradition, they were taken to Constantinople, and in 1204 they were brought to Venice and deposited in the monastery of St. George. But there is another tradition that they were brought to Metz by the emperor Otto I (936–973).

Lent

Along with the new feast days, there were also new fast days. The primitive rule prescribed fasting on Wednesdays and Fridays (although the Wednesday fast did not remain in force), and on the vigil of Easter. As early as the third century in some places, the Easter fast was extended to the six week-days of Holy Week.[38] By the fourth century a Lenten season of forty days was observed everywhere. There seemed to be a reference to Lent in the fifth canon of the Council of Nicaea (325), which ordered the bishops in each province to meet twice a year, "before the Fortieth" and again in the fall.[39] But that may actually be the fortieth day *after* Easter, later known as the feast of the Ascension, since the same ruling in the *Apostolic Constitutions* specified that the first of those meetings should be held during the fourth week of the Easter season.[40]

Whatever the Council of Nicaea had in mind, the Lenten season was definitely mentioned five years later in the second festal letter of St. Athanasius. It was the custom in Egypt for the patriarch to announce the date of the Easter festival in a letter issued on the Epiphany. In his first festal letter, Athanasius only mentioned the fast of Holy Week, but his letter for the year 330 gave the dates for the beginning of the fast of forty days and for the beginning of Holy Week.[41] Lent began six weeks before Easter, and so the forty days included Holy Week. Ten years later, however, Athanasius was complaining that the Egyptians were not actually observing the Lenten fast, and they were the only ones in the whole world not observing it.[42] Since he was living in exile in Rome at the time (one of many exiles from Alexandria), he could speak with some authority about the usages of other churches.

If the Lenten fast was not very popular in Egypt, there is nevertheless some evidence that a fast of forty days, in imitation of the fast of Jesus, had been kept there at an earlier period, not before Easter but after Epiphany.[43] In a church following the gospel of Mark, and celebrating the baptism of Jesus on the Epiphany, the fast of Jesus would follow immediately. According to Mark, after Jesus was baptized in the Jordan, "At once the Spirit drove him out into the desert, and he remained in the desert for forty days, tempted by Satan" (Mk 1:12). The connection between the two events is also clear in Matthew 4:1 and Luke 4:1. Of course a fast beginning on January 7 would only be possible in a church that celebrated the baptism of Jesus on January 6, and therefore not in Rome or in Jerusalem.

Although the Lenten fast is always known as the Forty Days (Quadragesima), the churches have never been able to agree about the exact length of the Lenten season or the precise manner of fasting. The simplest arrangement would be a Lent of six weeks, which would come to exactly forty days plus the Easter triduum. In the fifth century, the Byzantine historian Socrates claimed that Rome had a shorter Lent: "Those at Rome fast three successive weeks before Easter, excepting Saturdays and Sundays."[44] But as a matter of fact, there *was* fasting on Saturdays in Rome, which raises some doubts about the rest of the statement.

A Lent of six weeks was certainly the general custom in the west, but since fasting was forbidden on Sundays, there were only thirty-six days of actual fasting, including Good Friday and Holy Saturday. For that reason the beginning of the fast was moved back to the previous Wednesday (Ash Wednesday), without changing the official beginning of Lent on the following Sunday. These additional fast days are usually dated from the seventh century, but may actually be older than that. They were never added to the Lenten liturgy of the Ambrosian rite in Milan.

In the east there was no fasting on Saturdays or Sundays, except for Holy Saturday. Strictly speaking, therefore, forty days of fasting would require a Lent of eight weeks, and that was the Lent described by Egeria in the Jerusalem of the late fourth century. The same arrangement was tried, for a time, at Antioch and elsewhere. But the eastern churches generally preferred a Lent of seven weeks, that is, six weeks plus Holy Week, which was not included in the forty days. That would come to thirty-six days of actual fasting (including Holy Saturday), the same number as in the west before the addition of the four extra days. The *Apostolic Constitutions* had required a definite break between Lent and Holy Week, and the present Byzantine rite still has two festal days (Lazarus Saturday and Palm Sunday) before the fast of Holy Week.[45] Actually the first Sunday of Lent in both the Roman and Byzantine rites falls on the same day, the sixth Sunday before Easter, but the Lenten fast begins on the previous Monday in the Byzantine rite and on the previous Wednesday in the Roman rite. In the Greek church, from the seventh century, a modified fast was prescribed for the eighth week before Easter, known as Cheese-Fare Week.

In most churches the Lenten season was used to prepare candidates for baptism and for public penance. The scrutinies, or exorcisms of the catechumens, took place in Rome on the third, fourth and fifth Sundays of Lent. In 1972, after centuries of disuse, they were revived in the Rite of Christian Initiation of Adults. The reconciliation of penitents took place on Holy Thursday, according to Pope Innocent I in a letter written in 416.[46] They probably began their penitential exercises on the Monday after the first Sunday of Lent, when the gospel of the last judgment was read (Mt 25:31–46), a reading still used in the present Roman rite. This service was later transferred to Ash Wednesday. Both services, for the expulsion and for the reconciliation of penitents, were printed in modern editions of the Roman Pontifical, even though they were now only historical curiosities.

Ember Days

In Rome, from the late fourth century, fasting was also prescribed at the beginning of the summer, fall and winter.[47] With the Lenten fast in the spring, these were the fasts of the four seasons (*quattuor tempora* in Latin, ember days in English). The usual fast days (Wednesday, Friday and Saturday) were observed in each of the designated weeks. After some variation in the earlier period, the spring ember days were assigned to the first week of Lent, the summer ember days to the octave of Pentecost, the fall ember days to the week after September 14, and the winter ember days to the third week of Advent. The Ember Saturdays (particularly those in December) became the usual days for ordinations; the vigil service began on Saturday night and ended on Sunday morning.[48] From Rome the ember days were brought to the other churches of the west, but were not adopted by the eastern churches. In modern times the obligation of fasting on the ember days was removed in 1966, and the liturgical observance was abolished in 1969 (the local conference of bishops was authorized to make alternative arrangements).

Bishops could also order a fast for some special reason, at a time of impending disaster. Around 470 Bishop Mamertus of Vienne in Gaul instituted the rogation days on the three days before the feast of the Ascension, and this was made an annual observance in Gaul and eventually in Rome.[49] Evidently the idea of fasting during the Easter season was now acceptable. A procession was also ordered on each of the three days. The Roman church had a similar procession on April 25, known as the greater litanies. It replaced the pagan festival of the Robigalia and followed the same route on the Via Flaminia to the Milvian Bridge before turning toward St. Peter's. The greater litanies were retained even after the rogation days were imported from Gaul in the time of Pope Leo III (795–816). In 1969 both the rogation days and the greater litanies were removed from the general calendar (along with the ember days), and the assignment of days of special prayer was left to the local conference of bishops. Neither the rogation days nor the greater litanies were observed as fast days in Rome.

Advent

The fast before Christmas, known as Advent, probably originated in Gaul. Bishop Perpetuus of Tours (460–490) imposed an extra fast day, along with Wednesday and Friday, from the feast of St. Martin on November 11 until Christmas.[50] This "St. Martin's Lent" of six weeks was like the fast before Easter, but not as rigorous. Later regulations indicate that the extra day was Monday, not Saturday as in Rome. The Advent season was adopted in Rome in the late sixth century, but there it was reduced to four weeks, and there was less emphasis on fasting. The original six weeks of Advent are retained in the Ambrosian rite of Milan.

While the Advent season was obviously a time of preparation for Christmas, it also acquired an eschatological dimension, that is, an emphasis on the second coming of Christ at the end of the world, and for that reason a more penitential emphasis. This development has been attributed to the influence of the Irish missionaries in Gaul (e.g. St. Columban).[51] They used the season to urge the faithful to do penance before the coming of Christ at the last judgment. And so the penitential rites of Lent were transferred to Advent in the churches of Gaul, and to a lesser extent in Rome. The fasting regulations for Advent were finally abolished in the Code of Canon Law of 1917 (c. 1252). The Greek church has never had an Advent season as such, but they have had a pre-Christmas fast since the eighth century.

Dedications

By the fifth century it was customary to celebrate the anniversary of the dedication of churches, if the date was known. Even earlier, the buildings on Golgotha in Jerusalem had been dedicated on September 13, 335, and this feast of Dedication, or Encaenia, was kept as a major holy day, with an octave. Fifty years later Egeria described the celebration in her travel diary.[52] The biblical precedent was the dedication (Hanukkah) of the temple by Judas Maccabeus in 164 B.C., which was celebrated for eight days (1 Mac 4:36–59). Jesus visited the temple on the feast of the Dedication (Jn 10:22–23). The Dedication of the Church of the Resurrection is still celebrated in the Byzantine rite, but not in the Roman rite.

In Rome the dedication of the oldest churches (the Lateran basilica, St. Peter's and St. Paul's) was not celebrated until the eleventh century; presumably the date was not known. But later dedications were recorded, such as the dedication of St. Mary Major on August 5 by Pope Sixtus III (432–440), and St. Peter in Chains on August 1, also by Sixtus III. The dedication day of a church named in honor of a saint often became the feast day of that saint when the saint's date of death was not known. That would explain the dates of several feasts of the Virgin Mary and the apostles. Originally the mass on the dedication day was the mass in honor of the titular saint; that is still the case today on the dedication day of St. Mary Major (August 5) and Sts. Peter and Paul (November 18). In most cases, however, that has been replaced by a special mass for the Dedication of a Church. The custom of celebrating the dedication feast for eight days (the octave) was abolished in 1955, along with most of the other octaves.

THREE

The Early Middle Ages

Roman Stational Liturgy

It was customary in Rome, as in other large cities, for the bishop to celebrate mass in each of the city churches (known as *tituli*) during the course of the year. There were twenty-five of these churches in Rome in the fifth century. Pope Gregory the Great (590–604) revived the practice, and Pope Gregory II (715–731) added other churches to the schedule. There were eventually eighty-seven "station days," held at forty-two different churches. On the great festivals the station was assigned to one of the major basilicas, the Lateran or St. Peter's or St. Mary Major. The station days in the eighth-century schedule remained basically unchanged down to modern times, and were noted in the Roman Missal until 1969.[1]

In the fourteenth century the popes moved their residence to Avignon in France for seventy years, and when they returned to Rome there was little interest in reviving the stational visits. Like other bishops, the popes usually celebrated mass in their private chapel except on the greater feast days.

Nevertheless it was useful to have the stational churches listed in the missal, not only for historical reasons, but because the mass texts were often composed for that particular church. For example, the story of Susanna and the elders (Dan 13 in the Latin Vulgate) was read on the Saturday in Lent III because the station on that day was at St. Susanna, the former *titulus* of Gaius. Of course they were two different Susannas, but it seemed appropriate anyway. On Thursday of that week the cure of Peter's mother-in-law was read (Lk 4:38–44), because the station was at Sts. Cosmas and Damian, the physician saints, in what had been a pagan temple. Even though it was a Lenten mass, in the opening prayer it was called the "solemnity of Saints Cosmas and Damian." All these topical references have been removed from the Roman Missal of 1970, along with the stational information.

The ancient *tituli* had been named after their founders, but by the seventh century it was customary to name churches in honor of some saint, and so many of the *tituli* were given new names. In some cases, however, the original founder was simply converted into a saint, and a suitable legend was invented. No doubt these pious founders were "saints" in the wider sense, even if their legends were fictitious. So, for example, the *titulus* of Pudens, or *ecclesia Pudentiana,* became the church of St. Pudentiana, involving in this case a change of sex. Her feast was on May 19. Or a real saint was found who happened to have the same name as the *titulus.* In that way St. Chrysogonus of Aquileia was honored at the *titulus* of Chrysogonus, the Roman founder. His feast was on November 24. All but one of these saints were removed from the general calendar in 1969. An exception was made for St. Cecilia, the patron saint of musicians, named for the *titulus* of Cecilia (feast on November 22). Her legend was no more reliable than the others, but her popularity was greater.

Among the other saints whose cult is now limited to their titular churches are St. Anastasia (December 25), St. Praxedes (July 21), St. Eusebius of Rome (August 14), St. Cyriacus (August 8), St. Marcellus (January 16), St. Mark (October 7), St. Sabina (August 29), and St. Prisca (January 18). The beautiful church of St. Sabina was the stational church for Ash Wednesday; Pope Honorius III (1216–1227) gave it to St. Dominic as the church of his religious order.

A few saints whose names were later assigned to the *tituli* have been retained in the present Roman calendar, e.g. Sts. Nereus and Achilleus (May 12) and Sts. Marcellinus and Peter (June 2). The church of Sts. Cosmas and Damian was not one of the original *tituli,* but dates from the sixth century; their memorial on September 27 (probably the dedication day) was moved to September 26 to make room for the memorial of St. Vincent de Paul.

But some of these later dedications are no longer included in the general calendar, e.g. Sts. John and Paul (June 26), the Four Crowned Martyrs (November 8), and St. Susanna (August 11). St. Vitalis, the patron saint of the famous basilica in Ravenna, was assigned to the *titulus* of Vestina in Rome, and had two separate feast days, on April 28 and November 4. The first was removed from the calendar in 1960, and the second in 1969. Actually both feasts of St. Vitalis had previously been reduced to commemorations, to make room for St. Paul of the Cross on April 28 and St. Charles Borromeo on November 4.[2]

The trend to name churches in honor of saints even extended to the Lateran basilica, the cathedral church of Rome and the oldest of the great basilicas. It had originally been dedicated to the Holy Savior, but the adjoining baptistry was later provided with chapels in honor of St. John the Baptist and St. John the Evangelist. It was therefore known as St. John Lateran. Nevertheless the medieval and modern calendars continued to mark the dedication day on November 9 as the "Dedication of the Basilica of the Holy Savior." In the Roman Missal of 1970 this was changed to the "Dedication of the Lateran Basilica," probably because that was a more familiar title. The American editors of the liturgical books chose to make it even more familiar by calling it the "Dedication of Saint John Lateran," but the Roman authorities did not go that far.

Further Development of the Christmas Season

Originally the stational church for Christmas Day was St. Peter's. But in the fifth century a midnight mass was added at the Liberian basilica (St. Mary Major). In 431 the Council of Ephesus had affirmed the divine maternity of the Virgin Mary, and this may have inspired Pope Sixtus III (432–440) to give the church a Marian dedication. The additional mass may have been an imitation of the Epiphany services in Jerusalem: the bishop celebrated a midnight mass at the church of the Nativity in Bethlehem and then returned to Jerusalem for a morning mass in the Martyrium.[3] In Rome a third mass was added in the sixth century, a mass at dawn at the church of St. Anastasia. The cult of St. Anastasia of Sirmium was popular in Constantinople and in the Byzantine colony in Rome, and her name was attached to the fourth century *titulus* of Anastasia, in the Palatine district. When the church at large adopted the three Christmas masses, a commemoration of St. Anastasia was made at the second mass, but it was dropped from the Roman Missal of 1970. The third mass of Christmas was still scheduled at St. Peter's; it was eventually transferred to St. Mary Major by Pope Gregory VII (1073–1085).

In Rome January 1 was kept as the octave of Christmas (with a certain Marian emphasis), and not the feast of the Circumcision, as it was known in Gaul. Two commemorations were added, one of St. Basil (under Byzantine influence) and the other of St. Martina. The church of St. Martina in the Forum was built on the site of the senate archives, adjoining the curia; it is now known as the church of Sts. Luke and Martina. Although Martina was supposed to be a Roman martyr, with the usual fictitious legend, there is some doubt about her existence.

The Pre-Lenten Season

During the sixth and seventh centuries a pre-Lenten season was adopted throughout the Christian world. In the west this was known as Septuagesima from the name given to the first of the pre-Lenten Sundays, followed by Sexagesima and Quinquagesima, marking the (approximately) seventy, sixty and fifty days before Easter. The penitential rites associated with Lent, such as the suppression of the Alleluia, were now extended to Septuagesima. This season was abolished in the reformed Roman calendar of 1969.

In the Byzantine rite the Sunday of the Pharisee and the publican was assigned to the tenth Sunday before Easter, followed by the Sunday of the prodigal son (Septuagesima Sunday), meat-fare Sunday and cheese-fare Sunday. Meat-fare Sunday was followed by a week of semi-fasting, and the strict fast began on the week after cheese-fare Sunday. In the Greek church, however, the Alleluia was sung even during Lent.

The Lenten Liturgy

Throughout this period the Lenten services in Rome retained their primitive simplicity. The dramatic and the emotional were alien to Roman worship. The prestige of the Roman rite led to its adoption by the Frankish and Germanic peoples of the north in preference to the so-called Gallican rites, but they added to it those dramatic and emotional elements that satisfied their own religious needs. In 785 Pope Hadrian I (772–795) sent to Charlemagne the Roman sacramentary he had requested for use in the Frankish kingdom, but by the eleventh century a mixed Roman-Frankish-

Germanic liturgy was imposed on Rome itself.[4] The Greek church also had some influence in Rome, especially in the seventh and eighth centuries when several of the popes were of eastern origin.[5] The reforms of the Council of Trent (1545–1563) and the Second Vatican Council (1962–1965) were both attempts to restore the "noble simplicity" of the old Roman rite. It is therefore necessary to distinguish between the very few developments in Rome itself and the very many developments elsewhere.

On Ash Wednesday, for example, the Romans sang the antiphon "Let us change our garments for sackcloth and ashes," but the use of real ashes originated in northern Europe, and was not incorporated into the papal liturgy until the thirteenth century.[6] In the same way, the Roman sacramentaries referred to the Sunday before Easter as "Palm Sunday of the Lord's Passion" (the title restored in 1969), or simply "Palm Sunday," and in some places there was a procession with real palms by the ninth century, if not sooner. (In Jerusalem, of course, the procession with palms dates from the fourth century.) There was a procession in Rome in the eleventh century, "but the papal liturgy never gave it any great attention. The pope was satisfied to distribute blessed palms in a chapel of the Lateran palace, after which the procession descended to the basilica by the shortest way."[7] In Rome, therefore, Palm Sunday was devoted primarily to the reading of the passion in St. Matthew, to be continued with the story of the resurrection at the mass of the Easter vigil. A second liturgy of the word, with a second gospel, was later added for the blessing of palms. In the Greek church, on the contrary, the only gospel reading on Palm Sunday was the story of Christ's entrance into Jerusalem (Jn 12:1–18).

Holy Week

During Holy Week in Rome there were the usual prayer services on Wednesday and Friday. At the Good Friday service, in the church of the Holy Cross "in Jerusalem," the passion in St. John was read. The austere papal liturgy had no more than that in the seventh century, but in the eighth century (probably under eastern influence) the veneration of the cross was added. Elsewhere in the west, and in the parish churches of Rome, it was customary to receive communion from the reserved sacrament.[8] In the Greek church the Office of the Burial of Christ was sung on Good Friday.

The prayer of the faithful on Good Friday included a prayer for the unbelieving Jews (Pro perfidis Judaeis). In the ninth century, because of hostility toward the Jews, the usual genuflection was omitted for that prayer, and was only restored in the reformed liturgy of Holy Week in 1955.[9] Pope John XXIII (1958–1963) removed the word *perfidis* from the prayer, since it was often translated as "perfidious." An entirely new prayer was provided for the Roman Missal of 1970.

In Jerusalem and elsewhere, a mass of the Lord's Supper was celebrated on Holy Thursday in the fourth century.[10] In Rome, however, Holy Thursday was the day for the reconciliation of the penitents. By the seventh century there was a stational mass at the Lateran basilica for the blessing of the holy oils. In the Gelasian sacramentary there were three masses: for the reconciliation of penitents, for the blessing of the oils, and for the Lord's supper. In the Gregorian sacramentary these were combined in a single mass, but the liturgical reforms of 1955 provided for a separate chrism mass for the blessing of the oils.[11] As the Holy Thursday liturgy became more elaborate, and was shifted into the morning hours, this day was thought of as the first day of the sacred triduum, which no longer included Easter Sunday.[12]

After the mass of the Lord's Supper, the sacrament was carried in procession to a side chapel where it was kept for the communion service on Good Friday. Then vespers were recited, and the altars were stripped of their coverings. Finally, in cathedrals and monasteries, the washing of the feet was performed as the choir sang the antiphon "Mandatum novum do vobis" (Jn 13:34)—hence Maundy Thursday in English. These ceremonies reached Rome around the twelfth century. The stational church was the Lateran basilica, which was also the station for Palm Sunday and the Easter vigil, while the second Easter mass was at St. Mary Major.

The Easter Vigil

The Easter vigil in Rome, in its original form, was also a very simple service: nothing more than a vigil of prayer and fasting before the Easter mass. The earliest addition was the celebration of baptism, toward the end of the vigil and before the mass. Even that may not have originated in Rome, but may have been imported from elsewhere, like the rest of the ceremonial. But once the Easter vigil had become a baptismal service, it *remained* a baptismal service, even if there was no one to be baptized. That has never changed. In the Greek church, on the other hand, practically all associations with baptism had disappeared from the rite by the eleventh century.[13]

A second addition to the Easter vigil was the elaborate blessing of the paschal candle, going back to the fourth century in many parts of the church. The singing of the *Exsultet* was the oldest element; the grains of incense in the candle, marking it with the current year, etc., were not part of the original rite and are now treated as optional.

A third addition was the blessing of the new fire, struck from flint and used to light the paschal candle and the other lights in the church. The candle was then carried into the church in a procession that halted three times for the singing of the *Lumen Christi.* This rite was added to the Roman liturgical books in the twelfth century. In the thirteenth century a three-branched candle was used in the procession, and was later used to light the paschal candle. A simplified version of this rite (without the three-branched candle) is still in use.

During the early middle ages the Easter vigil, and all other vigil masses, were gradually moved back to an earlier hour of the afternoon, and finally into the morning. On a fast day mass was supposed to be celebrated after the office of None, at three o'clock. But then None itself was moved back to the morning, and the mass was moved with it. Even though the Easter vigil mass was still officially the first mass of Easter Sunday, it was followed by a short service of vespers which replaced the usual post-communion prayers. Then it seemed necessary to add an office of Matins and Lauds for Sunday, which was actually a second vigil service before the second Easter mass. When the reforms of 1951 restored the Easter vigil to its original time, a short office of Lauds was said at the end. This was replaced in 1970 by a separate office of Lauds (morning prayer) for Easter Sunday morning.

In the Greek church the Easter vigil suffered the same fate: it was read (officially) as a service of vespers combined with the divine liturgy of St. Basil. It was actually moved back to Saturday morning, and the only reminder of its former baptismal function was the antiphon sung after the last of the fifteen Bible readings: "For all of you who were baptized into Christ have clothed yourselves with Christ" (Gal 3:27). But the second Easter mass was also moved back, from Sunday morning to midnight, preceded by an office of Matins and Lauds. In other words, the old Easter vigil was replaced by a new one in the same time period. Therefore the Byzantine rite churches do not need any reforms in their Easter services, except perhaps a shorter liturgy, and that is actually done informally in the parish churches.

Pentecost

The feast of Pentecost, the last day of the Easter season, acquired all the privileges of an independent feast day, at least in the west. By the end of the fourth century Pentecost (also known as Whitsunday) was an alternative day for baptism, with a vigil service copied from the Easter vigil. Like the Easter vigil, the vigil of Pentecost was eventually moved back to Saturday morning. The baptismal rite was abolished in 1955, leaving only the vigil mass. By the sixth century the old rule that there should be no fasting during the Easter season was breaking down, and the vigil became a fast day. It remained one of the four fasting vigils (with the Assumption, All Saints and Christmas), at least officially, until the reforms of 1966.[14]

Like other feast days, Pentecost also acquired an octave, although that prolonged by a week what was supposed to be the *end* of the Easter festival.[15] The octave clashed with the summer ember days, mixing feast days with fast days in the same week, a situation that survived the reforms of 1955, and was finally resolved in 1969, when both the octave *and* the ember days were abolished.

For the Sundays after Pentecost, a series beginning on different dates every year (May 17 to June 20), there were various arrangements. In some lectionaries they were numbered consecutively from the first to the twenty-fourth. In others they were grouped in relation to the nearest feast day, e.g. five Sundays after Pentecost, five after Sts. Peter and Paul, six after St. Lawrence, one *dominica vacans,* and eight after St.

Michael the Archangel.[16] The consecutive numbering won out, with twenty-four Sundays after Pentecost and six Sundays after Epiphany (plus the three Sundays of Septuagesima), based on a late date for Easter. When Easter came earlier, the Sundays not needed after Epiphany were inserted between the twenty-third and twenty-fourth Sundays after Pentecost, so that the mass of the twenty-fourth Sunday was always the last before Advent. This system remained in force until the reform of the Roman calendar in 1969. No provision was made for masses on weekdays, except for the Lenten season, the octaves of Easter and Pentecost, and the ember days. The reading of the Bible in the course of the year was assigned to the office of Matins.

The Holy Cross

The feast of the Exaltation of the Holy Cross was celebrated in Jerusalem in the fifth century, and had reached Rome by the seventh century. Originally the Dedication of the Holy Sepulcher and the finding of the cross of Jesus were celebrated together on September 13, but by the fifth century there was a separate feast of the Holy Cross on September 14.[17] In Rome, however, that date was the feast of Sts. Cornelius and Cyprian, and so the two feasts were combined until the fourteenth century, when Pope Gregory XI (1370–1378) transferred the two martyrs to September 16.

There was a good deal of interest in the holy cross in the seventh century, since the Persians had sacked Jerusalem in 614 and captured the cross. But in 628 the emperor Heraclius defeated the Persians, and the cross was then returned to Jerusalem, except for a portion sent to Constantinople. (Relics of the cross had been sent to many places, including Rome, during the previous centuries.) It was the recovery of the cross by

Heraclius that was celebrated by the Roman feast of September 14, while the Finding (*Inventio*) of the Holy Cross was celebrated on May 3. The legend of the finding of the cross by St. Helena goes back at least to the year 395, when it was mentioned by St. Ambrose.[18] May 3 was also the feast of the martyrs Alexander, Eventius, Theodulus and Juvenal, and so the two feasts were combined until 1960, when the Finding of the Cross was dropped from the Roman calendar, and 1969, when the martyrs were also dropped. The Finding of the Cross is still celebrated in Brazil (where it is a patronal feast), in Mexico and elsewhere.

Marian Feasts

A feast in honor of Mary the Mother of God (*Theotokos*) was celebrated in Jerusalem on August 15, according to the fifth century Armenian Lectionary.[19] The original site was at the place "where the Virgin rested" between Jerusalem and Bethlehem, where a church had been built.[20] By the end of the fifth century the feast was being celebrated at the tomb of the Virgin in Gethsemane, and was therefore known as the Dormition of Mary. It became the principal feast of Mary throughout the Christian world.

The feast of the Nativity of Mary on September 8 may be the dedication day of the church of St. Anne in Jerusalem, the traditional site of Mary's birth. And the Presentation of Mary on November 21 may be the dedication day of New St. Mary's in Jerusalem in the year 543, on the south side of the temple (now the Al-Aqsa mosque). The story of the presentation of Mary in the temple is found in the apocryphal *Protoevangelium of James.*[21]

In Rome the Marian feasts were celebrated from the seventh century. The octave of Christmas on January 1 celebrated Mary's divine motherhood, like the Commemoration of Mary in the Greek church on December 26. It has sometimes been called the first feast of Mary in the Roman church, but if so, it was soon overshadowed by the great eastern festivals.[22]

Until the fourteenth century there were only four Marian feasts in the Roman calendar: the Nativity (September 8), the Annunciation (March 25), the Purification (February 2) and the Assumption (August 15).[23] Two of those, the Annunciation and the Purification (Presentation), were really feasts of our Lord, but were regarded as Marian feasts until the reforms of 1969. That left the feasts of Mary's Nativity and Assumption, both derived from the Jerusalem calendar. Pope Sergius I (687–701), of Syrian background, ordered processions to St. Mary Major on the four feasts.

There was some hesitation at first about the feast of the Annunciation, since it fell in Lent. In Rome the gospels of the annunciation and visitation were read on the Wednesday and Friday of the December ember days (since 1969 on December 20 and 21). In Spain there was a Marian feast on December 18, and in Milan on the Sunday before Christmas. In 692 the Council *in Trullo* of the Greek Church (canon 52) made the feast of the Annunciation the one exception to the rule forbidding feast days in Lent.[24] In the Byzantine rite (but not in the Roman) it is celebrated even when it falls in Holy Week.

The feast of the Presentation or Purification on February 2, commonly known as Candlemas, is the only one of the four feast days still celebrated with a procession. It was always customary to carry candles in the procession, but a blessing of candles did not appear in the Roman books until the twelfth century. The words of the *Nunc dimittis,* "A light of revelation to the Gentiles, and glory for your people Israel" (Lk 2:32), are sung in the procession and in the gospel of the mass.

The nativity or birth of Mary was not recorded in the Bible, and therefore there was no obviously suitable gospel reading. The Roman church used the genealogy of Jesus (Mt 1:1–16). The Roman Missal of 1970 added part of the story of the birth of Jesus (Mt 1:18–23), as an addition to the genealogy or as a substitute for it. In modern times this feast, which had been second in importance only to that of the Assumption, has been replaced in that position by the Immaculate Conception (December 8). So, for example, it was not included among the holy days of obligation in the Code of Canon Law of 1917 (canon 1247, 1), or the Code of Canon Law of 1983 (canon 1246, 1).

The feast of the Assumption of Mary also lacked an obviously suitable gospel reading. The curious choice in the old Roman rite was the story of Martha and Mary of Bethany (Lk 10:38–42). When the doctrine of the assumption was defined in 1950, an entirely new mass was composed. The gospel of the visitation was used, with part of the Magnificat (Lk 1:41–50). In the Roman Missal of 1970 it was lengthened to include the whole Magnificat (Lk 1:39–56). For the vigil mass the old gospel reading was retained: "Blessed is the womb that bore you" (Lk 11:27–28).

In the Greek church the same gospel readings were used for the Nativity of Mary and the Dormition or Assumption, and provided the readings for the Assumption in the west. They combined the story of Martha and Mary of Bethany (Lk 10:38–42) and "Blessed is the womb that bore you" (Lk 11:27–28). For the feast of the Assumption in Rome, the first part was used for the gospel of the day and the short second part was used on the vigil.

On the four Marian feasts the processions to St. Mary Major set out from the church of St. Hadrian in the Forum. This church occupied the former curia of the senate, next door to the senate archives, which had been converted into the church of St. Martina (now Sts. Luke and Martina). St. Hadrian was a martyr of Nicomedia whose feast was celebrated in Rome on September 8, along with the Nativity of Mary. In 1937 the church of St. Hadrian was demolished to allow for the restoration of the curia, and in 1969 his name was removed from the general calendar.

Other Feasts

The cult of St. George in Rome was associated with the seventh century diaconal church of St. George in Velabro. Although nothing is known about him except for his martyrdom at Diospolis (Lydda) in Palestine, the legends about him made him popular with soldiers. In the wake of the crusades he was made patron saint of England. His memorial on April 23 is retained in the Roman calendar.

St. Valentine, a Roman martyr, was buried on the Via Flaminia, where a church was built in the fourth century. However the Roman martyrology, on February 14, has an entry for another Valentine, also a martyr, who was the bishop of Terni, fifty miles north of Rome. Whether they were two different persons, or one person with two different legends, is still debated. In any case, St. Valentine has only an accidental connection with the sending of love letters. That is usually traced back to the medieval belief that the mating season for birds began in mid-February, i.e. February 14. In 1969 that day was assigned to the memorial of Sts. Cyril and Methodius instead of St. Valentine.

A great many of the (mostly Roman) martyrs are no longer found in the general calendar since the reform of 1969. In many cases they had already been displaced by more recent saints, but were still allowed a commemoration. Now their memorials are restricted to local calendars or their titular churches. Not counting those added in the later middle ages, the following ancient memorials were abolished in 1969:

JANUARY
1. Martina (January 30 in modern calendars)
14. Felix of Nola (not a martyr)
16. Marcellus, pope (not a martyr)
18. Prisca
19. Marius, Martha, Audifax and Abachum
23. Emerentiana

FEBRUARY
14. Valentine

MARCH
Feast days in Lent were generally avoided. Sts. Perpetua and Felicity (March 7) are retained in the present calendar.

APRIL
14. Tiburtius, Valerian and Maximus
28. Vitalis

MAY
3. Alexander, Eventius and Theodulus; Juvenal of Narni
10. Gordian and Epimachus
19. Pudentiana
25. Urban I, pope (not a martyr)—probably a different Urban
31. Petronilla

JUNE
9. Primus and Felician
12. Basilides, Cyrinus, Nabor and Nazarius
15. Vitus

18. Mark and Marcellian
19. Gervasius and Protasius
26. John and Paul
30. Commemoration of Paul the Apostle

JULY
 2. Processus and Martinian
10. The Seven Holy Brothers
21. Praxedes
23. Apollinaris of Ravenna
29. Felix, Simplicius, Faustinus and Beatrice
30. Abdon and Sennen

AUGUST
 1. The Maccabees; St. Peter's Chains
 2. Stephen I, pope (not a martyr)
 7. Donatus of Arezzo (not a martyr)
 8. Cyriacus, Largus and Smaragdus
11. Tiburtius and Susanna
14. Eusebius
18. Agapitus of Palestrina
22. Timothy and Symphorian
28. Hermes
29. Sabina
30. Felix and Adauctus

SEPTEMBER
 8. Hadrian of Nicomedia
 9. Gorgonius
11. Protus and Hyacinth
15. Nicomedes
16. Euphemia of Chalcedon; Lucy and Geminian
20. Eustace

OCTOBER
7. Mark, pope (not a martyr)
25. Chrysanthus and Daria

NOVEMBER
8. The Four Crowned Martyrs
9. Theodore of Amasea in Pontus
11. Mennas of Alexandria
23. Felicity
24. Chrysogonus of Aquileia
29. Saturninus

DECEMBER
2. Bibiana
25. Anastasia of Sirmium

New Saints: The Eighth Century

By the eighth century a few "confessors" were being admitted to the liturgical calendars. Originally the confessors were those who had suffered for the faith during the persecutions, but had not been put to death. Later the title was given to any saint who was not a martyr. St. Martin of Tours, who died in 397, was one of the first confessor-saints, and was honored in Rome in the sixth century. But at least in Rome only a few other confessors were honored as saints during the following centuries. They were mainly bishops and, later, abbots.

Among these confessors was Pope Sylvester I (314–335), the first bishop of Rome after the conversion of Constantine and the end of the persecutions. His feast was on December 31, during the octave of Christmas, now reduced to a commemoration. His life was the subject of legends as early as the fifth century, and he later figured prominently in the famous forgery known as the "Donation of Constantine."[25] Oddly enough he was listed in medieval calendars as a martyr.

The antipope Felix II (355–365) somehow got into the church calendar as a saint and, through confusion with another Felix, as a martyr. When Liberius, the legitimate pope, was banished by the emperor Constantius II, who favored the Arian heresy, Felix was installed as his successor. Three years later Liberius was allowed to return, but Felix managed to retain the loyalty of some of the Romans until his death in 365. Later tradition identified Felix as the legitimate pope and Liberius as the intruder, and his feast day was celebrated on July 29, the feast of St. Felix, a Roman martyr. He was officially recognized as an antipope in 1947, but there was no change in the liturgical books until 1969, when the name of Felix on July 29 was removed from the calendar. Even now, however, the popes who came after him, and had the same name, are usually listed as Felix III and Felix IV, not to mention another antipope known as Felix V (1439–1449).

Pope Leo the Great (440–461), who saved Rome from Attila the Hun, died on November 10. He was originally commemorated on the day of the translation of his remains to St. Peter's: June 28. That was in 688, under Pope Sergius I. In the Gallican books his feast was on April 11, which became the Roman date in the twelfth century. It was moved to November 10 in 1969. The old feast of Pope Leo on June 28 was associated with Pope Leo II (682–683). In 1921 it was moved to July 3, the day when Leo II died, and in 1960 it was removed entirely.[26] St. Irenaeus was responsible for both changes: in 1921 he was assigned to June 28, and in 1960 he was moved to July 3 (in 1969 he was restored to June 28). June 28 also happened to be the vigil of the apostles Peter and Paul, but that is now observed only as an optional evening mass.

Pope Gregory the Great (590–604) died on March 12, which was always his feast day, despite the fact that it fell in Lent. He is still commemorated on that day in some places, but in 1969 his memorial in the Roman calendar was moved to September 3, the day of his ordination as bishop of Rome. The Roman Martyrology had an entry on both dates: on March 12 he was called the Apostle of the English for sending St. Augustine of Canterbury on a mission to England, and on September 3 he was called "that incomparable man . . . who shone out on the world from his sublime throne with ever clearer rays of sanctity."[27] Like Pope Leo the Great, Gregory was originally buried in the vestibule of St. Peter's; his remains were transferred to the basilica itself in 1606. His feast has been celebrated in Rome since the eighth century.

Until the end of the middle ages there were only four doctors of the church: Gregory the Great, Ambrose, Augustine and Jerome. All except Ambrose were commemorated in Rome by the eighth century. St. Ambrose, the great bishop of Milan, died on April 4, 397. His feast was often kept on that day during the middle ages, and later in the Anglican Church. But since it usually coincided with Holy Week or Easter Week (he actually died on Good Friday), in Milan and in the Roman and Greek churches it was transferred to December 7, the anniversary of his ordination as bishop. In Rome that date had been kept as the Octave of St. Andrew, but it was eventually yielded to St. Ambrose. In 1879 Pope Leo XIII allowed the vigil of the Immaculate Conception to be celebrated on December 7, as an optional alternative to the feast of St. Ambrose, but the vigil was abolished in 1955.

St. Augustine, the last of the great African bishops, died on August 28, 430. In Rome that was the feast day of St. Hermes, a Roman martyr, and so the two saints shared the day until 1969, when the commemoration of St. Hermes was eliminated. The remains of St. Augustine were brought from

Africa to Sardinia, and in the eighth century were transferred to Pavia, where they are now enshrined in the church of St. Peter.

St. Jerome, the patron saint of biblical studies, died in Bethlehem on September 30, 420. In Rome, under Pope Damasus, he had worked on the Latin translation of the Bible, but after the death of Damasus in 384 he retired to a monastery in Bethlehem. His body was later brought back to Rome, and is said to be somewhere in the church of St. Mary Major.

St. Benedict, the abbot of Monte Cassino and the father of western monasticism, died sometime around the year 547. There is a French tradition that his relics were transferred to Fleury in the diocese of Orléans in the seventh century, but the claim was contested by Monte Cassino. His cult was slow in developing. His feast was celebrated either on March 21 or on July 11. From the eleventh century it was kept in Rome on March 21, but in 1969 it was transferred to July 11 to move it out of Lent. The Benedictines usually celebrate both days: the *Transitus* on March 21 and the Solemnity or Translation or secondary feast on July 11. In 1964, twenty years after the destruction of Monte Cassino in the Second World War, Pope Paul VI consecrated the restored monastery and named St. Benedict the patron saint of Europe.

New Saints: The Ninth Century

During the ninth century several feasts of apostles were added to the few found in the old Roman calendar. The reason for the dates chosen is usually not known, but most of them were assigned to the season after Pentecost. Despite their late appearance in the calendar, they became important holy days in the middle ages.

St. James the Greater, the brother of St. John and the first of the apostles to die for the faith, was commemorated on July 25 (April 30 in the Greek church). King Herod Agrippa "had James, the brother of John, killed by the sword" (Acts 12:2). But Spanish legends claimed that he had preached in Spain, and that his relics were later brought to Compostella; the shrine of Santiago became one of the great goals of medieval pilgrims.

St. Bartholomew the Apostle was listed in medieval calendars on August 25 (the Greek date) or August 24. The preference in Rome was for August 25, but in the fourteenth century that became the feast of King Louis IX, who died on that day in 1270. Since the sixteenth century St. Bartholomew has been commemorated by Catholics and Protestants on August 24. The Greek church also has a feast of Sts. Bartholomew and Barnabas on June 11, which is the feast of St. Barnabas alone in the west. The relics of St. Bartholomew were believed to be in Benevento around the year 1000, when they were taken to Rome by the emperor Otto III and deposited in the church of St. Bartholomew on the Tiber Island. It is possible, however, that the "real" relics were kept in Benevento.[28]

The feast of St. Matthew the Apostle was celebrated on September 21 (November 16 in the Greek church). His supposed relics are in the cathedral of St. Matthew in Salerno. The cathedral was built by the Norman Robert Guiscard and consecrated by Pope Gregory VII shortly before his death in 1085. The pope's tomb is in the cathedral.

St. Luke the Evangelist was commemorated on October 18 in both the Roman and Greek churches. He supposedly died in Greece, and his relics were brought to Constantinople by the emperor Constantius II (337–361) and deposited in the church of the Apostles. In Rome the church of St. Martina in the Forum is now known as Sts. Luke and Martina because Pope Sixtus V (1585–1590) assigned it to the Academy of Fine Arts, whose patron saint was St. Luke.

The apostles Simon and Jude were commemorated together on October 28; in the Greek Church the feast of St. Simon the Zealot was on May 10 and that of St. Jude Thaddeus on June 19. Of the various legends about them, the west evidently accepted the one that had them martyred together in Persia. Their feast day may be the day of the translation of their reputed relics to St. Peter's in Rome. The devotion to St. Jude in the Catholic Church is a modern development: in 1929 the Claretian Fathers founded the League of St. Jude in Chicago, where they built the National Shrine of St. Jude.

Until recently the feast of St. Thomas the Apostle was on December 21 (October 6 in the Greek church). But the Roman Martyrology had a notice on July 3 of the translation of his relics to Edessa. The tradition that he preached the gospel in India is still maintained by the St. Thomas Christians of India, although they agree with the other Syrian churches in celebrating July 3 as the anniversary of his death. The translation to Edessa at the end of the fourth century was supposedly followed by other moves and finally to Ortona in Italy, where the cathedral is dedicated to St. Thomas. The Roman feast day on December 21 was the only saint's day in December, except for St. Lucy, before Christmas. In 1969 the feast of St. Thomas was moved to July 3 so that the special masses provided for the week before Christmas would not be interrupted.

The ninth century also saw the adoption in the west of All Saints Day on November 1. In the Greek church All Saints Day was celebrated on the first Sunday after Pentecost, an observance going back to the fourth century. In Rome Pope Boniface IV consecrated the Pantheon as a Christian church on May 13 around the year 609 and dedicated it to all the martyrs. It was known as Santa Maria ad Martyres. November 1 may be the dedication day of a chapel in St. Peter's dedicated to all the saints by Pope Gregory III (731–741).[29] Pope Gregory IV (827–844) asked Emperor Louis the Pious, the son of Charlemagne, to have the feast celebrated throughout the empire. In Rome November 1 was already assigned to St. Caesarius, a martyr of Terracina; he was still allowed a commemoration in the medieval calendars. But the adoption of All Saints Day on November 1 caused the disappearance of the older feast day on May 13. The vigil of All Saints Day, known in England as All Hallows Even or Halloween, was abolished in 1955.

All Souls Day on November 2 dates from the year 998, when St. Odilo, the abbot of Cluny, ordered prayers for all the dead on that day. The devotion spread rapidly throughout northern Europe, but was not accepted in Rome until the fourteenth century. The custom of offering three masses on All Souls Day began in Spain, and was approved for that country in 1748. In 1915 during the First World War, Pope Benedict XV extended the privilege to all the clergy.[30] The Greek church has a commemoration of the faithful departed twice a year: on the Saturday of Meat-Fare Week and on the Saturday before Pentecost.[31]

Finally, the feast of the Conversion of St. Paul on January 25 was borrowed from the Gallican rite. The date was the octave day of St. Peter's Chair, which the Gallican church celebrated on January 18 to keep it out of Lent (the Roman feast of St. Peter's Chair was on February 22). Both feasts are kept only in the western church. The epistle for January 25 in the old Roman Missal was from Acts 9:1–22; now there is a choice between that and Acts 22:3–16.

The tenth century was a dark age. Rome now received back from the German emperors the liturgy that had been sent to northern Europe in the days of Charlemagne, with the adaptations that made it a Roman-Frankish-German liturgy. While these adaptations were extensive, they did not affect the basic structure of the church year. There were few, if any, changes in the calendar.

New Saints: The Eleventh Century

The expansion of the church calendar was resumed in the eleventh century. The feast of St. Matthias the Apostle on February 24 (August 9 in the Greek church) completed the roster of the twelve apostles. Matthias was the replacement for Judas (Acts 1:15–26). His relics were supposedly brought from Jerusalem to Rome by St. Helena, and in the eleventh century some of them were taken to Trier in Germany, where they were enshrined in the church of St. Matthias (the only tomb of an apostle north of the Alps). In 1969 his feast day was moved to May 14 to avoid the Lenten season, but the old date was retained in the German calendar. The new date has no particular significance, except that it is around the time of the ascension, when Matthias was elected.

St. Mark the Evangelist was the last of the four evangelists to be given a feast day: on April 25. In Rome the greater litanies were held on that day, and until they were abolished in 1969 there was a double celebration. In Egypt St. Mark was regarded as the founder of the church of Alexandria. In the ninth century his reputed relics were taken to Venice, where he was venerated as the patron saint of the city. There is a fourth century church of St. Mark in Rome, in what is now the Palazzo Venezia. The relics of Sts. Abdon and Sennen were brought there by Pope Gregory IV (827–844).

St. Barnabas (June 11) was also venerated as an apostle, but not one of the twelve. The same title was given to his companion, St. Paul (Acts 11:21–26 and 13:1–3).

The feast of St. Denis (Dionysius), the first bishop of Paris, and his companions was celebrated on October 9. In the ninth century he was identified, incorrectly, with two other individuals: Dionysius the Areopagite, a disciple of St. Paul (Acts 17:34), and the author of several books on mystical theology who was believed to be the Areopagite, but actually wrote sometime around the year 500. The martyrdom of St. Denis of Paris is usually dated around the year 250.[32] The basilica over his tomb became the place of burial of the kings of France; in the twelfth century it was the first great Gothic structure.

Another patron saint of Paris was St. Genevieve, a nun who died around 500. Her feast on January 3 is celebrated in France, but was not added to the Roman calendar. King Louis XV built a new church over her tomb, but after the French Revolution it became the secular Pantheon. In 1793 her relics were exhumed and burned. Today the shrine of St. Genevieve is in the neighboring church of St.-Etienne-du-Mont.

The feast of St. Nicholas (December 6) became very popular in the west after the translation of his relics to Bari, Italy in 1087. Nothing is really known about him except that he was the bishop of Myra in Asia Minor in the fourth century. Nevertheless he became the patron saint of sailors and children and pawnbrokers, and of entire countries like Greece and Russia. Construction of the basilica of St. Nicholas in Bari began immediately after the translation of his relics, and the feast of the translation is celebrated there on May 9. It is also celebrated in the Byzantine rite.

Pope Gregory VII (1073–1085), in his *Dictatus papae* on the authority of the pope, claimed in article 23 that "the Roman pontiff, if canonically ordained, is undoubtedly sanctified by the merits of St. Peter."[33] But in fact very few popes have been canonized, and not all of the canonized popes were admitted to the general calendar. The Philocalian Calendar of 354 listed only four bishops of Rome among the martyrs: Callistus (217–222), Pontian (230–235) and Hippolytus the anti-pope, Fabian (236–250), and Sixtus II (257–258). Cornelius (251–253), who died in exile, was later recognized as a martyr and, since his date of death was not known, was assigned to the feast day of his colleague St. Cyprian of Carthage.

That was originally on September 14, but was moved to September 16 by Pope Gregory XI (1370–1378) because of the feast of the Holy Cross on September 14 and the octave of the Nativity of Mary on September 15.

Clement of Rome, who is usually counted as the third bishop of Rome after Linus and Cletus, was the author of the Epistle to the Corinthians. In later legend, he was exiled to the Crimea, where he was put to death and thrown into the sea. Angels placed his body in an underwater tomb. His reputed relics were returned to Rome by Sts. Cyril and Methodius, who presented them to Pope Hadrian II (867–872). They were deposited in the church of St. Clement, one of the oldest churches in Rome. His feast day was celebrated on November 23.

These, and a few others, like Sylvester I, Leo the Great and Gregory the Great, were the only popes venerated as saints during the first ten centuries. Eventually thirty-eight popes would be admitted to the general calendar, but twenty-six of them were from the early period when the church was being persecuted. In the middle ages they assumed that all the popes from that period were martyrs, and therefore saints. Even so, it took about three hundred years to complete the project of adding those names to the Roman calendar.

In the eleventh century feast days were assigned to St. Linus (September 23), St. Evaristus (October 26), and St. Pius I (July 11), although their actual anniversaries were not known. Pope Damasus I (366–384), who had done so much to promote the cult of the Roman martyrs, was himself honored as a saint on December 11. Pope Martin I (649–655) condemned the Monothelite doctrine favored by the emperor Constans II, who accused him of treason and banished him to the Crimea. He died there as a result of the harsh treatment he was given: the last of the martyr-popes. His feast day was on November 12, the day after the feast of St. Martin of Tours, but in 1969 it was assigned to April 13, which seems to be his actual anniversary (it is also his feast day in the Byzantine calendar).

By the eleventh century a feast of dedication was being celebrated for the ancient Roman basilicas of the Lateran, St. Peter's and St. Paul's. That had long been the custom for other churches, but they had been built before there was such a custom. The dedication of the Lateran basilica was celebrated on November 9, and the dedication of St. Peter's and St. Paul's was combined on November 18. Since 1969 the latter has been an optional memorial in the general calendar, but the dedication feast for the Lateran basilica is celebrated even when it falls on a Sunday. The new St. Peter's was consecrated on November 18, 1626. But when St. Paul's was destroyed by fire in 1823, the new building was consecrated by Pope Pius IX on December 10, 1854. Nevertheless there was no change in the traditional dedication day. There was a change, in 1969, in the mass for November 18. Instead of the mass for the dedication of a church, it is now a mass in honor of the apostles Peter and Paul (the more ancient custom for a dedication feast).

During the earlier centuries the saints were often provided with fictional biographies, but the saints themselves were usually real people. That was not always the case in the medieval period. The early Christians knew perfectly well that the *Acts of Paul and Thecla* were apocryphal, but St. Thecla, the fictional convert of St. Paul, had a feast day on September 23 (with Pope Linus) until 1969. She still has a memorial on September 24 in the Byzantine calendar.[34]

St. Maurice and Companions, formerly commemorated on September 22, were supposedly soldiers of the Theban legion who were put to death at Agaunum, now Saint-Maurice-en-Valais in Switzerland. This story may well have a basis in fact, even if the number of martyrs was much less than the six thousand and more of the legend. Their feast is still celebrated in Switzerland and various other places.

St. Erasmus, bishop of Formiae, was formerly commemorated on June 2 with Sts. Marcellinus and Peter. In the ninth century, when Formiae was attacked by the Saracens, his remains were transferred to the nearby town of Gaeta. It replaced Formiae as the episcopal see, and adopted St. Erasmus as its patron saint. He became, like St. Nicholas, a patron saint of sailors, and gave his name, in its Italian form, to the electrical discharge known as St. Elmo's fire.

FOUR

The Later Middle Ages

The Twelfth Century

The Roman calendar of the twelfth century showed a notable increase in the number of feast days, even though "modern" saints were generally excluded. When St. Thomas Becket, the archbishop of Canterbury, was canonized in 1173, only three years after his death, the most recent entry before that was for Pope Gregory the Great, who died in 604. "Up to the thirteenth century, it is evident, the Middle Ages only went on repeating the old data and rather parsimoniously exchanging some feasts between one local church and another."[1]

One of the reasons for these additions to the calendar was the custom of reading the martyrology every day in cathedrals and monasteries. The more interesting saints could be transferred from the martyrology to the church calendar, and thanks to the legends of the saints, many of them were interesting. Furthermore the martyrologies tried to be all-inclusive, listing every known saint of the eastern and western churches. The Hieronymian, or martyrology of St. Jerome, dating from the fifth century, combined material from Roman, African and eastern sources, and became the source for later martyrologies. In the eighth century the Venerable Bede compiled a martyrology that included some biographical information about the saints, a practice followed by his successors. His work was continued in the ninth century by an anonymous author of Lyons and by Florus of Lyons. Then, around 860,

Ado of Vienne revised their work without much regard for historical truth. Many of the dates were incorrect. A few years later Usuard of Saint-Germain used Ado's martyrology as the basis for his own, and that in turn became the principal source for the Roman martyrology of modern times.[2] The resulting errors in the identity of the saints and their feast days were finally corrected in the reformed calendar of 1969.

The opinion of Pope Gregory VII (1073–1085) that all popes should be honored as saints was never taken too seriously, but many of them were added to the Roman calendar during the eleventh, twelfth and thirteenth centuries. All the popes of the first three centuries were honored as saints and martyrs, although most of them were *not* martyrs, and until the mid-third century there were no authentic records of the date of death or burial. The feast days for the earlier popes were assigned to the dates found in the *Liber Pontificalis,* which was believed to be a reliable source.[3] The *Liber Pontificalis* was also responsible for the assignment of separate feast days for Cletus (April 26) and Anacletus (July 13), two names for the same person, an error finally corrected in 1960.

Almost all the popes down to Felix IV (526–530) were regarded as saints, but not all of them were given feast days. From the sixth to the ninth centuries, there were only a few saints and even fewer feast days: only Gregory the Great and (later) the martyr-popes Silverius and Martin I. After the ninth century there were none at all. Pope Leo IX (1049–1054) was honored as a saint in Rome and in Germany, but not in the general calendar. In 1294 the hermit Peter of Morrone was elected pope as Celestine V, but he resigned the papacy a few months later. He was canonized in 1313, as a hermit, not as a pope, and his feast was not added to the general calendar until 1668 (it was suppressed in 1969).[4]

Therefore Pope Martin I, who died in 655, was the last pope to receive liturgical honors until the eighteenth century.

In 1712 Pope Pius V (1566–1572) was canonized, and in 1728 the name of Pope Gregory VII was added to the calendar, more than six hundred years after his death. Finally, Pope Pius X (1903–1914) was canonized in 1954. Obviously the church cannot be accused of favoritism on behalf of the papacy in the canonization of saints.

Other additions to the calendar in the twelfth century included the following:

JANUARY
1. Basil the Great was commemorated on the feast of the Circumcision, as in the Greek church, but in the thirteenth century his feast was moved to June 14, the date found in the martyrology of Ado.
10. Paul the First Hermit. His feast was later moved to January 15th, as in the Greek church.
15. Maurus, disciple of St. Benedict. He was confused with another Maurus, abbot of Glanfeuil in France, whose anniversary was kept on this day.
17. Anthony of Egypt, venerated as the founder of the monastic life.
22. Anastasius the Persian, a martyr of the seventh century.

FEBRUARY
3. Blase was supposedly the bishop of Sebaste in Armenia and a martyr of the fourth century, commemorated in the Greek church on February 11. His legend has no historical basis, but his memorial was retained in the Roman calendar because of the popular blessing of throats in honor of St. Blase.
10. Scholastica, the sister of St. Benedict.

MARCH
9. The Forty Martyrs of Sebaste were soldiers who were ex-

posed naked on a frozen lake. Their cult was very popular in the east. In 1649 the feast was moved to the following day to make room for the feast of St. Frances of Rome.

JUNE

22. Paulinus of Nola, the bishop of Nola in Campania, died in 431. The emperor Otto III (983–1002) brought his relics to Rome, where they were placed in the church of St. Bartholomew on the Tiber Island. Pope Pius X returned them to Nola in 1909.

JULY

17. Alexis, the man of God, apparently existed only as the hero of the story who left home on his wedding night and returned years later to live unknown as a beggar in his father's house. In the Greek church his feast is on March 17.

22. Mary Magdalene was usually identified with Mary of Bethany and with the sinner who anointed the feet of Jesus (Lk 7:37–50). In the western legends, Mary, Martha and Lazarus preached the gospel in Provence, France. The abbey of Vézelay claimed to have the relics of Mary Magdalene, but they were also claimed by Saint-Maximin in Provence. The gospel for the feast was formerly the story of the sinner, but it is now the story of the appearance of the risen Christ to Mary Magdalene in John 20:1–2, 11–18.

The twelfth century additions to the July calendar also included several feasts of martyrs, e.g. Rufina and Secunda (10), Nabor and Felix (12), Symphorosa and her seven sons (18), Pantaleon or Panteleimon (27), and Nazarius and Celsus (28). St. Panteleimon, the holy physician, was a popular eastern saint.

SEPTEMBER

1. Giles was supposedly the founder of a monastery in Provence, but even the century in which he lived is not known. His legends were completely fictitious and very popular.

OCTOBER

7. Sergius and Bacchus, officers in the Roman army, were martyred at Rosafa in Mesopotamia, later known as Sergiopolis. In Rome October 7 was also the feast of Pope Mark, and later of Sts. Marcellus and Apuleius (supposedly converts of St. Peter the Apostle), and still later of the Holy Rosary. To relieve the crowding, the four martyrs were moved to the following day in 1960, and were removed from the general calendar in 1969.

NOVEMBER

26. Peter of Alexandria, bishop and martyr, was commemorated on November 24 in the Greek church, on November 25 in Egypt and in Russia, and on November 26 in the Roman calendar.

DECEMBER

4. Barbara was supposed to be a virgin-martyr of the early church, but even her existence has been questioned. In some military forces, she is still honored as patron saint of the artillery. In the Byzantine calendar St. Barbara and St. John of Damascus are commemorated together. In the Roman calendar St. John of Damascus replaced St. Barbara in 1969.

5. Sabbas, abbot of the monastery of Mar Saba in Palestine, died in 532. Mar Saba is one of the oldest functioning monasteries in the world. Monks driven from Mar Saba in the seventh century founded the church of St. Sabbas

in Rome. The saint's relics were taken to Venice, but were
returned by Pope Paul VI in 1965. His feast was removed
from the Roman calendar in 1969, but is still celebrated
by the Benedictines and Cistercians.

29. Thomas Becket, archbishop of Canterbury, was mur-
dered in his cathedral in 1170. He was canonized three
years later, and his feast was immediately added to the
Roman calendar. The translation of his relics to a shrine
in the cathedral in 1220 was celebrated on July 7 (later
restricted to the Catholic diocese of Portsmouth). His
shrine was one of the great goals of medieval pilgrimages.
It was destroyed by King Henry VIII, who ordered the
removal of his feast day from the Anglican calendar.

The Thirteenth Century

Canonization by the pope would affect the church calendar in ways not anticipated by the papacy. Formerly the veneration of holy men and women as saints depended on the
wishes of the local church and its bishop. Popes were sometimes asked to intervene, as in the canonization of Bishop
Ulric of Augsburg in 993 by Pope John XV, the earliest docu-
mented example. The word "canonize" was first used by Pope
Alexander III in 1173, for St. Thomas Becket. In 1174 he
canonized St. Bernard of Clairvaux, who died in 1153.

Alexander III had to contend with several antipopes, and
one of them, Paschal III, authorized the canonization of
Charlemagne in 1166. He did so at the behest of the emperor
Frederick Barbarossa, his patron, who wished to strengthen
his position against Alexander III. While the acts of an antipope could be considered invalid, and there is no evidence
that Charlemagne was ever venerated as a saint before 1166,
nevertheless a feast in his honor was permitted in Aachen,
where he is buried.[5]

By the thirteenth century papal canonization had become the rule rather than the exception. One of the unexpected results of this new procedure was to increase the number of saints, especially "modern" saints, in the general calendar. Saints who had been canonized locally were usually venerated locally, except for the most popular saints, like Martin of Tours. Saints canonized by the pope had a much better chance of being admitted to the Roman calendar and to all the calendars of the western church. In fact the popes sometimes gave orders to that effect, e.g. for the feast of St. Francis of Assisi. And since requests for canonization came from all over Europe, the Roman calendar became less and less "Roman."[6]

The new religious orders also affected the church calendars. These international orders needed a uniform liturgy with an international calendar.[7] The Franciscans adopted the liturgy of the papal court, which suited their needs better than the ceremonial of the Roman basilicas. By the sixteenth century the whole western church (with some exceptions) would be using that liturgy, with a universal calendar.[8] The Dominicans, who had their own distinctive rite, based their calendar on the ninth century Gregorian sacramentary, to which they added a sufficient number of non-Roman saints to make it an international calendar.[9]

From the very beginning the Dominicans were more restrained than the Franciscans in adding new feast days. In April, for example, the Franciscans of the thirteenth century celebrated fourteen feast days, the Dominicans only six. At that early stage the two orders had only a few saints of their own. In fact the only friar in the two April calendars happened to be a Dominican martyr, Peter of Verona. But the Franciscans were using the calendar of the papal court, which listed thirteen popes in April (several of them were paired on the same day), while not a single pope was listed for that month in the Dominican calendar. In modern times, however, even the Dominicans welcomed new feast days for the saints of the order: more of them were added to the calendar during the nineteenth century and the first half of the twentieth than in all the previous centuries.[10]

The feast days added to the Roman calendar during the thirteenth century included the following:

JANUARY
13. Hilary of Poitiers, the defender of the Catholic faith against the Arians, died around 367. In medieval calendars his feast was combined with the octave of the Epiphany on January 13. In England it began the Hilary Term in the law courts and universities. In Rome it was transferred to the following day, but was restored in 1969.
24. Timothy, the disciple of St. Paul, was venerated as the first bishop of Ephesus. In the Greek church his feast day was on January 22, according to legend the day of his martyrdom. His supposed relics were brought to Constantinople in 356. In the west his feast day was celebrated on the day before the Conversion of St. Paul. In 1969 it was moved to January 26, with St. Titus, the other disciple of St. Paul (the feast of St. Titus only dates from 1854).
26. Polycarp, the bishop of Smyrna, was martyred on February 23, c. 155, according to the account of his martyrdom written by the witnesses. In the east his feast was celebrated on that day, but in the west it was assigned to January 26, the feast of another saint named Polycarp. In 1969 it was moved to the correct date.
27. John Chrysostom, bishop of Constantinople and one of the great doctors of the church, died on September 14, 407, the feast of the Holy Cross. He had been sent into exile by the emperor Arcadius, and died of exhaustion on the journey. His remains were brought back to Constan-

tinople in 438, and the feast of the Translation was celebrated on January 27. In the east his principal feast is on
November 13, and in the Roman calendar (since 1969)
on September 13.

FEBRUARY

1. Ignatius of Antioch, the bishop of that church, was
brought to Rome to be thrown to the lions, probably
around the year 107. The Greek church commemorated
his death on December 20, and the translation of his remains to Antioch on January 29. The Roman date came
from Ado's martyrology. In 1969 it was moved to October 17, his feast day in the church of Syria since the
fourth century.

Brigid of Kildare, one of the most famous of the
saints of Ireland, was also commemorated on February 1
in most western calendars, including the Roman.

4. Gilbert of Sempringham was the founder of the Gilber-
tines, the only medieval religious order founded in England. Most of the members were nuns, with some priests
(canons regular) and lay brothers. Gilbert died in 1189
and was canonized soon after, in 1202. The order became
extinct when Henry VIII suppressed the English monasteries. The feast of St. Gilbert was dropped from the Roman calendar, but was kept in two English dioceses.

6. Dorothy seems to have been a martyr of Caesarea in Cappadocia. Her legend was popular in the west, and her
reputed relics were enshrined in the church of St. Dorothy
in Rome. She is not commemorated in the Byzantine
calendar.

9. Apollonia was a martyr of Alexandria during the persecution of Decius, around 249. Bishop Dionysius of Alexandria wrote an account of her martyrdom, in which she

was described as an elderly deaconess. She is not commemorated in the Byzantine calendar.

15. Faustinus and Jovita were honored as martyrs and patron saints of Brescia in northern Italy.

JUNE

13. Anthony of Padua, born in Lisbon, Portugal, was one of the early followers of St. Francis of Assisi. He served as a teacher and preacher in the order, and died at the age of thirty-six, in 1231. He was canonized the following year. In Padua he is simply "il Santo." In 1946 he was included among the doctors of the church.

JULY

20. Margaret of Antioch was apparently a fictional character whose legend was very popular in the middle ages. In the east she was venerated as St. Marina on July 17. Her feast was dropped from the Roman calendar in 1969.

24. Christina of Tyre in Phoenicia seems to have been another fictional character, commemorated on this date in the Greek church. In the west she was identified with a probably genuine martyr of Bolsena, Italy. Her feast was also dropped from the Roman calendar in 1969.

26. Ann was the mother of the Blessed Virgin Mary (and Joachim was her father) in the apocryphal books of the early church. The emperor Justinian (527–565) built a church in her honor in Constantinople, where her feast was celebrated on July 25. In the west her feast was celebrated on the following day, since July 25 was the feast of St. James, beginning in the thirteenth century. It was dropped from the Roman calendar in 1568, but was restored in 1584. The feast of St. Joachim, dating from 1584, was celebrated on various days, but in 1969 was combined with the memorial of St. Ann. In the Greek church Joachim and Ann were commemorated together on September 9, the day after the Nativity of Mary.

The shrine of Sainte-Anne-de-Beaupré in Quebec was founded in 1658; the church, rebuilt in 1876, was entrusted to the Redemptorists in 1878.

29. Martha of Bethany, the sister of Mary and Lazarus, was commemorated in the Franciscan calendar from 1262, and soon after in the Roman calendar. The date chosen was the Octave of St. Mary Magdalene, who was identified with Mary of Bethany. It is now celebrated as the memorial of Martha, Mary and Lazarus in the Benedictine and Cistercian calendars.

AUGUST

5. Dominic, the Spanish founder of the Order of Preachers, died at Bologna, Italy, on August 6, 1221. A church was built over his tomb, and he was canonized in 1234. Since August 6 was the feast of Pope Sixtus II, his feast day was assigned to August 5. In Rome the Dedication of St. Mary Major was celebrated on August 5, along with the feast of St. Dominic, but in 1558 Pope Paul IV decided to move St. Dominic to August 4. There was great resentment among the Dominicans, who did not accept the change until the following century.[11] In 1969 his memorial was moved again, this time to August 7 (briefly), and then to August 8.

In the Dominican Order, the Translation of St. Dominic in 1233 is celebrated on May 24.

12. Clare of Assisi, who founded the Franciscan order of nuns known as the Poor Clares, died on August 11, 1253. She was canonized two years later, and her feast was assigned to August 12, the day of her burial. In 1969 it was moved to August 11.

20. Bernard of Clairvaux, the great saint of the Cistercian

Order of monks, died in 1153 and was canonized in 1174. But his feast was not added to the Roman calendar until the thirteenth century. In 1830 he was named a doctor of the church.

22. The ancient memorial of St. Timothy, a Roman martyr, was combined in the thirteenth century with the memorials of St. Hippolytus, "bishop of Porto," and St. Symphorian, a martyr of Autun in Gaul. This Hippolytus seems to be the same person as the third century antipope who died a martyr and was commemorated with Pope Pontian on August 13. In 1969 their memorial was replaced by the Queenship of Mary (formerly the octave of the Assumption).

25. Louis IX, king of France, died at Tunis in 1270, on his second crusade. He was canonized in 1297. In Rome the feast of St. Bartholomew the Apostle was celebrated on August 25, but was later moved to the previous day.

SEPTEMBER

1. The Twelve Brothers were not really brothers, but martyrs in various towns in Italy. Their relics were deposited in the church of St. Sophia in Benevento in the eighth century. In Rome their memorial was combined with that of St. Giles, but both were removed from the general calendar in 1969.

26. Cyprian and Justina were apparently purely fictional characters in a legend about their martyrdom. As early as the fourth century, the fictional Cyprian was being confused with the real Cyprian of Carthage. Their feast was removed from the Roman calendar in 1969, but is still found in the Byzantine calendar on October 2.

OCTOBER

1. Remigius, bishop of Rheims and apostle of the Franks,

baptized Clovis, king of the Franks (481–511). He died on January 13, 533, but his translation was celebrated on October 1. In France his memorial is now celebrated on January 15.

4. Francis of Assisi, the founder of the Order of Friars Minor, died in 1226 and was canonized two years later. His feast was immediately added to the Roman calendar. The feast of the Stigmata of St. Francis (September 17), no longer in the general calendar, is still celebrated by the Franciscans. In 1939 St. Francis and St. Catherine of Siena were made patron saints of Italy.

21. Hilarion, an abbot in Palestine, died in Cyprus around 371. St. Jerome wrote his biography. His memorial was removed from the Roman calendar in 1969, but is still kept on this day in the Byzantine calendar.

NOVEMBER

4. Vitalis and Agricola were believed to be Christian martyrs whose remains were discovered in Bologna in 393. St. Ambrose was one of the witnesses. Their memorial was removed from the general calendar in 1969 (another feast of St. Vitalis on April 28 was removed in 1960).

6. Leonard was supposedly the founder of a monastery (now the town of Saint-Léonard) about twelve miles from Limoges. He was very popular in northern Europe, and was commemorated in the medieval Roman calendar and the Anglican Book of Common Prayer.

13. Brice (Britius) succeeded St. Martin as bishop of Tours in 397, and lived until 444. He was commemorated in the medieval Roman calendar and the Anglican Book of Common Prayer.

25. Catherine of Alexandria, according to her legend, was a virgin martyr whose body was carried by angels to Mount Sinai. Her feast was removed from the Roman calendar in 1969, but is still celebrated on this day in the Greek church and on the preceding day in the Russian church. The monastery of St. Catherine at Mount Sinai was built by the emperor Justinian (527–578).

The feast of the Holy Trinity was celebrated in many places by the thirteenth century, but not yet in Rome. A mass of the Holy Trinity for use on Sundays was composed by Alcuin around the year 800. It was one of a set of votive masses for each day of the week. The idea of Sunday as a weekly feast of the Holy Trinity replaced the original significance of Sunday as a memorial of the resurrection. An annual feast of the Holy Trinity was popular in northern Europe, particularly in the monasteries. In Rome, however, Pope Alexander II (1061–1073) is reported to have said that there was no need for such a feast, since the church honors the Trinity every day.[12] It was also rejected by Pope Alexander III (1159–1181). But in 1334 Pope John XXII ordered it to be celebrated on the first Sunday after Pentecost. Even so, it was not raised in rank from a feast to a solemnity (using modern terminology) until 1911.

In northern Europe, where many churches were dedicated to the Trinity, the feast was often celebrated with an octave. And instead of numbering the Sundays "after Pentecost" (the Roman usage before 1969), they were numbered "after Trinity." The Lutheran and Anglican churches continued that practice after the reformation, as did some of the religious orders, such as the Dominicans.[13]

In the Byzantine rite, Pentecost itself is celebrated as a feast of the Holy Trinity. A commemoration of the coming of the Holy Spirit is made on the following day. The gospel for Pentecost, "On the last and greatest day of the feast" (Jn 7:37–52; 8:12), was chosen because it was the last day of the Easter festival.

The feast of Corpus Christi was accepted in Rome soon after it was first celebrated at Liège (Belgium) in 1247. As it happened, Pope Urban IV, who extended the feast to the whole church in 1264, had served as archdeacon of Liège. It was there that the nun Juliana of Mont-Cornillon had a vision in which the Lord asked for an annual feast in honor of the Blessed Sacrament. The part played by St. Thomas Aquinas in composing the mass and office of Corpus Christi is still being debated.[14] Despite the pope's decree, the feast of Corpus Christi was not generally accepted until the fourteenth century, when new decrees were published by Pope Clement V at the Council of Vienne (1311–1312), and Pope John XXII in 1317. The procession with the Blessed Sacrament, still customary in Catholic countries, was introduced during the fourteenth and fifteenth centuries. The day chosen for the feast was the Thursday after the octave of Pentecost, the first free Thursday after the Easter season. In countries where it is not a holy day of obligation, it is transferred to the following Sunday. The octave of Corpus Christi was abolished in 1955.

The Fourteenth Century

During the fourteenth century (the century of the black death), there were only a few additions to the church calendar. The Presentation of Mary on November 21 was apparently the dedication day of Santa Maria Nova (now a mosque) on the south side of the temple mount in Jerusalem. It was built by the emperor Justinian in 543. In the Greek church it became the feast of the Entrance of the Mother of God into the Temple, an event described in the apocryphal gospels. In the west Pope Gregory XI accepted the feast at Avignon in 1372.[15] It was rejected by Pius V in 1568, because of its apocryphal aspects, but was restored by Sixtus V in 1585. In Germany it was recently changed to the memorial of "Our Lady in Jerusalem."[16]

A feast of the Visitation of Mary on July 2 was adopted by the Franciscans in 1263. In the Greek church the Deposition of the Robe of the Virgin Mary in Blachernae, a church in Constantinople, was celebrated on July 2, and the gospel for the feast was the story of the visitation (Lk 1:39–56). It also happened to be the first day after the octave of John the Baptist. In 1389 Pope Urban VI accepted the feast in order to obtain Mary's help in ending the great schism. It was added to the general calendar in 1568. In 1969 it was moved to May 31 so that it would come before, instead of after, the birthday of John the Baptist (June 24).

Thomas Aquinas, the great Dominican theologian, died on March 7, 1274, at the Cistercian monastery of Fossanova, on his way to the Council of Lyons. He was canonized in 1323, and in 1368 his remains were translated to Toulouse, France. In 1567 Pope Pius V named him a doctor of the church. He was made patron saint of Catholic universities in 1880. In 1969, to avoid the Lenten season, his memorial was moved from March 7 to January 28, the anniversary of his translation.

The feast of St. Ursula and the Eleven Thousand Virgins on October 21 was derived from a popular legend. Ursula was supposedly a British princess who suffered martyrdom at Cologne, Germany, with her eleven thousand companions. Her name lives on in the Ursuline order of nuns founded by St. Angela Merici in 1535. The feast was removed from the Roman calendar in 1969.

The Fifteenth Century

There were also very few additions to the church calendar during the fifteenth century. The feast of the Transfiguration of the Lord was celebrated in the east from the fifth or sixth century. The date of August 6 may be the dedication day of a church on Mount Tabor, the traditional site of the transfiguration. It may also reflect the tradition that Jesus was transfigured forty days before the crucifixion, the latter represented by the feast of the Holy Cross on September 14.[17] Churches in the west celebrated the feast beginning in the ninth century. In 1457 Pope Callistus III added it to the Roman calendar to commemorate the Christian victory over the Turks at Belgrade a year earlier.

A feast of St. Ann's Conception of Mary on December 9 was celebrated in the Greek church from the eighth century. It was brought to England in the eleventh century, and later to France and other countries in the west (on December 8). There it was associated with the belief that Mary was conceived without original sin. There was opposition from St. Bernard and other theologians, but the Franciscans defended the feast, and in 1476 the Franciscan Pope Sixtus IV added it to the Roman calendar. It was raised in rank and given an octave in 1693, and made a holy day of obligation in 1708. After the definition of the doctrine in 1854, it became the feast of the Immaculate Conception. In 1879 it was again raised in rank to a feast of the first class (solemnity), with a vigil as an alternative to the feast of St. Ambrose. Both the octave and the vigil were abolished in 1955. The Immaculate Conception became the patronal feast of Spain and Latin America in 1760, and of the United States in 1846.[18]

St. Joseph, the husband of Mary, was commemorated in some medieval martyrologies on March 19, but the reason for the date is not known. The liturgical cult of St. Joseph dates from the fifteenth century, and was accepted in Rome by Pope Sixtus IV in 1479. His feast day was made a holy day of obligation in 1621. A second feast, the Patronage of St. Joseph, was assigned to the third Sunday after Easter in 1847. It was changed to the solemnity of St. Joseph, on the third Wednesday after Easter, with an octave, by Pope Pius X. In 1955 it was changed again, to the feast of St. Joseph the Worker on May 1 (celebrated as Labor Day in most countries).

St. Joseph was named patron saint of the universal church in 1870, and he is also honored as patron saint of Belgium and Canada. His principal shrine is the Oratory of St. Joseph in Montreal, Quebec, founded by Bl. André Bessette in 1904.

Bonaventure, the "second founder" of the Franciscans, died on July 15, 1274, at the Council of Lyons. He was canonized by Pope Sixtus IV in 1482, and his feast was added to the Roman calendar. He was named a doctor of the church in 1588.

During the first half of the sixteenth century, before the liturgical reforms of 1568, some additional names were added to the Roman calendar, mostly ancient saints who had somehow been overlooked. They were probably chosen, not because of popular devotion, but because they were admired by the humanists in the church. St. Athanasius, the bishop of Alexandria and the great defender of the Catholic faith against the Arians, died on May 2, 373. He was commemorated on that day in the east and in some medieval calendars in the west. His feast was added to the Roman calendar in 1550.

Monica, the mother of St. Augustine, died at Ostia in Italy in 387, but the day of death was not known. In the fifteenth century the Order of St. Augustine celebrated the Conversion of St. Augustine on May 5 and the feast of St. Monica on May 4. Her feast was added to the Roman calendar around 1550. In 1969 it was moved to August 27, the day before the feast of St. Augustine. (The Augustinians now celebrate the Conversion of St. Augustine on April 24th.) The church of St. Augustine in Rome, built in the fifteenth century, claims to have Monica's relics.

Gregory of Nazianzus, bishop of Constantinople and friend of St. Basil, known as Gregory the Theologian, died on January 25, 389 or 390. His feast was added to the Roman calendar around 1500 on May 9, the date found in Ado's martyrology. In 1969 it was moved to January 2 and combined with the feast of St. Basil.

Christopher, the patron saint of travelers, was commemorated in the Greek church on May 9, the feast of Isaiah the prophet. In the West he was commemorated on July 25th, the feast of St. James the Apostle. His name was removed from the Roman calendar in 1969, but is still found in local calendars (e.g. in Germany). Erasmus, in his *Praise of Folly,* mentioned the popular belief that anyone who looked at a picture of St. Christopher would not die that day.[19] For that reason a large picture of St. Christopher was provided in the vestibules of many medieval churches.

FIVE

The Reformation and the Council of Trent

The Protestant Reformers

Despite all their differences, the Protestant and Catholic reformers of the sixteenth century could at least agree that there were too many saints' days and too many abuses in the cult of the saints. There were the fake relics and other frauds, the ridiculous legends, and the saints for every need (one for toothaches and another for eye problems). There was the suspicion that the saints were taking the place of Christ as the "one mediator between God and men, the man Christ Jesus" (1 Tim 2:5). The Protestants took the further step of rejecting the invocation of the saints.

The Lutherans kept at least the feasts of the Lord (Christmas, Good Friday, Easter, Ascension and Pentecost), and the Augsburg Confession (article xxi) allowed for the commemoration of the saints, provided that prayers were not said to them. Some Lutheran churches did keep the feasts of the biblical saints (mainly the apostles and evangelists) in their calendars. John Calvin, however, rejected the saints' days completely, and his views prevailed in the Reformed churches.[1] Many churches abandoned the Christian year altogether, keeping only the Sunday worship. They could argue that even the feasts of the Lord lacked a scriptural warrant, and had been occasions for superstition or at least merrymaking.

In England the first Book of Common Prayer (1549) kept the feasts of the Lord and the biblical saints, plus All Saints

Day. There were no feasts of the Virgin Mary except the Purification and the Annunciation, which were really feasts of the
Lord. In the second Book of Common Prayer (1552), the feast
of St. Mary Magdalene was dropped and a few non-biblical
names were added to the calendar: St. George, St. Lawrence
and St. Clement. But no services were provided for those
saints. In the Book of Common Prayer of 1662 more than fifty
non-biblical saints were added to the calendar, including
many English saints, but again no services were provided.
Other entries (without services) were for the Conception, Nativity and Visitation of Mary, the two feasts of the Holy Cross,
the Transfiguration, and the Name of Jesus (August 7).

The Reforms of Trent

The Council of Trent, at the twenty-fifth session in 1563,
defended the invocation of the saints, the veneration of relics,
and the legitimate use of images. But it also demanded that the
abuses be corrected: "Furthermore, in the invocation of the
saints, the veneration of relics, and the sacred use of images,
all superstition shall be removed, all filthy quest for gain eliminated, and all lasciviousness avoided," and the festivals of
the saints should not be celebrated with revelry and
drunkenness.[2]

In 1568 the Dominican Pope Pius V published the reformed Roman calendar, which would now be the official
calendar of the whole western church (with some exceptions).
In response to the complaints about the excessive number of
saints' days, the Tridentine commissions went back to the
calendar of Pope Gregory VII in the late eleventh century.
Since that time about two hundred new feasts had been added
to the calendar. Only the most important of those were kept in
the reformed calendar. Even the Presentation of Mary (No-

vember 21) and the feast of St. Ann were dropped, but were later restored. There were now only 149 feast days, including octaves, of which about 130 were saints' days. As in the ancient calendar, most of the saints were martyrs, especially Roman martyrs. In fact, eighty-five percent of the saints were from the first four centuries. On the other hand there were only two saints each from France, England and Spain, and only one (the dubious St. Ursula) from Germany.[3] Those churches and religious orders using the Roman calendar could combine it with their own local calendars.

The Sixteenth Century

Although a Congregation of Rites was organized in 1588 to safeguard the Tridentine reforms, the invasion of the calendar by new feast days continued without interruption until the reform of 1969. By 1907 the 149 feast days of 1568 had increased to 280, and at least thirty more were added by 1969.[4] Even the calendar of 1568 added the name of St. Gregory the Wonderworker, bishop of Neocaesarea in Pontus, who died around 270. His feast was on November 17, as in the Greek church. Also the local Roman feast of the Dedication of St. Mary Major on August 5 was extended to the whole church as the feast of Our Lady of the Snow. And the feasts of the Presentation of Mary and St. Ann, dropped in 1568, were restored by 1585. In that year the Stigmata of St. Francis was added to the calendar on September 17.

From now on the influence of the old and new religious orders would account for many of the new feast days. It would obviously be gratifying if their saints were commemorated not only in the calendar of the order but also in the general calendar. Before the end of the sixteenth century they included the Dominican martyr St. Peter of Verona (April 29), the Benedictine St. Romuald, the founder of Camaldoli (June 19), the Benedictine St. John Gualbert (July 12), the Augustinian St. Nicholas of Tolentine (September 10), the Benedictine St. Placid (October 5), and the Franciscan St. Diego (November 12). All of these, except St. Romuald, were dropped from the 1969 calendar.

Another reason for the steady increase in the number of feast days had to do with the divine office. By ancient tradition, the book of Psalms was recited once a week. But on feast days the office was much shorter, with fewer and shorter psalms, and fewer prayers. The more feast days, the lighter the burden of the daily hours of prayer: Matins, Lauds, Prime, Terce, Sext, None, Vespers and Compline.

The Seventeenth Century

The additions to the Roman calendar during the seventeenth century included the following:[5]

JANUARY
5 Pope Telesphorus
7 Raymond of Peñafort
19 King Canute IV of Denmark
24 Francis de Sales
28 Peter Nolasco
30 Martina

FEBRUARY
4 Andrew Corsini
8 John of Matha

MARCH
4 Casimir and Pope Lucius

9 Frances of Rome
17 Patrick

APRIL
5 Vincent Ferrer
13 Hermenegild
21 Anselm of Canterbury

MAY
10 Antoninus
16 Ubaldus
18 Venantius
19 Pope Celestine V
20 Bernardine of Siena
25 Mary Magdalene de Pazzi
26 Philip Neri

JUNE
6 Norbert

JULY
4 Elizabeth of Portugal
13 Emperor Henry II
23 Bridget of Sweden
31 Ignatius of Loyola

AUGUST
2 Eusebius of Vercelli
7 Cajetan
16 King Stephen of Hungary
17 Hyacinth of Cracow
23 Philip Benizi
31 Raymond Nonnatus

SEPTEMBER
 5 Lawrence Justinian
12 Holy Name of Mary
22 Thomas of Villanova
24 Our Lady of Ransom
28 Wenceslaus of Bohemia

OCTOBER
 2 The Guardian Angels
 6 Bruno the Carthusian
10 Francis Borgia
13 King Edward the Confessor
15 Teresa of Avila
17 Hedwig
19 Peter of Alcantara

NOVEMBER
 4 Charles Borromeo
16 Queen Margaret of Scotland
17 Elizabeth of Hungary
20 Felix of Valois

DECEMBER
 3 Francis Xavier

The Eighteenth Century

The new feast days added during the eighteenth century included the following:

JANUARY
 2 The Holy Name of Jesus

FEBRUARY
 8 Jerome Emiliani

MARCH
 8 John of God

APRIL
 4 Isidore of Seville
24 Fidelis of Sigmaringen
30 Pope Pius V

MAY
17 Paschal Baylon
25 Pope Gregory VII

JUNE
12 John of Sahagun
19 Juliana Falconieri
25 William of Montevergine

JULY
14 Camillus de Lellis
16 Our Lady of Mount Carmel
23 Liborius of Le Mans
30 Peter Chrysologus

AUGUST
23 Rose of Lima
25 Joseph Calasanz

SEPTEMBER
18 Joseph of Cupertino
27 Vincent de Paul

OCTOBER
7 Our Lady of the Rosary

NOVEMBER
10 Andrew Avellino
16 Gertrude the Great

DECEMBER
12 Jane de Chantal
14 John of the Cross
23 John of Kanty

The scholarly Pope Benedict XIV (1740–1758), author of a classic work on the canonization of saints, was concerned about the invasion of the calendar by new feast days. He refused to make any further changes, except to name Pope Leo the Great a doctor of the church. And he ordered a revision of the Roman Breviary that would eliminate all the legendary material in it. However the project was never completed.

His successor, Pope Clement XIII (1758–1769), allowed the addition of new saints' days, and was the first pope to canonize six saints at the same time, in 1767: John of Kanty, Joseph of Cupertino, Joseph Calasanz, Jerome Emiliani, Seraphin of Montegranaro, and Jane de Chantal. All except St. Seraphin were added to the general calendar, and all except St. John of Kanty, a secular priest, were members of a religious order.

The Nineteenth Century

Almost all the feast days added during the nineteenth century (unlike those of the previous centuries) can still be found in the present Roman calendar:

JANUARY
26 Titus
27 Angela Merici

FEBRUARY
14 Cyril and Methodius
17 The Seven Founders of the Servites
21 Peter Damian

MARCH
18 Cyril of Jerusalem

MAY
25 The Venerable Bede
27 Augustine of Canterbury

JUNE
1 Justin Martyr
4 Francis Caracciolo
5 Boniface
21 Aloysius Gonzaga
27 Cyril of Alexandria

JULY
1 The Precious Blood of Jesus
5 Anthony Zaccaria

AUGUST
1 Alphonsus Liguori

SEPTEMBER
15 Our Lady of Sorrows

OCTOBER
19 Paul of the Cross
23 John of Capistrano

NOVEMBER
12 Josaphat
26 Sylvester Gozzolini

DECEMBER
 4 John of Damascus

An important addition to the calendar during the nineteenth century was the feast of the Sacred Heart of Jesus. Devotion to the Sacred Heart was promoted by the medieval mystics and later by the Jesuits, based on texts such as John 7:37 and 19:34. St. John Eudes, the French Oratorian, celebrated the first mass of the Sacred Heart in 1672. The visions of St. Margaret Mary Alacoque, a Visitation nun, called for a feast of the Sacred Heart. It was adopted in several countries, and was added to the general calendar in 1856. The date was the Friday after the Octave of Corpus Christi (the third Friday after Pentecost). Many different liturgies were composed for the feast, usually emphasizing either thanksgiving or reparation; both themes can be found in the present texts.[6]

In 1889 the feast of the Sacred Heart was made a solemnity (in modern terminology), and in 1929 it was given a new mass and office, and celebrated with an octave (later abolished). The basilica of the Sacred Heart in Paris, on Montmartre, was built after the French defeat in the Franco-Prussian War of 1870.

The Twentieth Century

The process of adding new feast days continued during the first half of the twentieth century, and almost all of them were retained in the calendar of 1969:

JANUARY
31 John Bosco

FEBRUARY
11 Our Lady of Lourdes
27 Gabriel Possenti

MARCH
24 Gabriel the Archangel

APRIL
7 John Baptist de la Salle

MAY
1 Joseph the Worker

JUNE
9 Ephrem the Syrian
17 Gregory Barbarigo
28 Irenaeus of Lyons

JULY
21 Lawrence of Brindisi

AUGUST
4 John Vianney

19 John Eudes
21 Pope Pius X
22 Queenship of Mary/Immaculate Heart

SEPTEMBER
17 Robert Bellarmine

OCTOBER
 1 Theresa of the Child Jesus
 9 John Leonardi
11 The Maternity of Mary
16 Margaret Mary Alacoque
24 Anthony Claret and Raphael the Archangel

NOVEMBER
15 Albert the Great

DECEMBER
21 Peter Canisius

In 1921 Pope Benedict XV added the feast of the Holy Family to the general calendar, on the first Sunday after Epiphany. The gospel from the Sunday mass, the finding of the child Jesus in the temple (Lk 2:42–52), was used for the feast. The devotion began in the nineteenth century, and was popular especially in Canada. In 1969 the feast was moved to the Sunday after Christmas.

In 1925 Pope Pius XI instituted the feast of Christ the King, to be celebrated on the last Sunday in October, the Sunday before All Saints Day. In 1969 it was moved to a more suitable date on the last Sunday in Ordinary Time (the Sunday before Advent). Since then it has been adopted by several other Christian churches.[7] But perhaps there can be too many feasts of the Lord, just as there can be too many feasts of the saints. In 1941 Father Jungmann suggested that "a feeling of weariness may come over us as we view these interminable expansions of the liturgical picture of Christ. Constant new enterprises, constant new images, constant new climaxes, constant new phraseologies."[8]

And in fact two feasts of the Lord were removed from the general calendar in 1969. The Franciscan feast of the Holy Name of Jesus was added to the general calendar in 1721, to be celebrated on the Sunday between January 1 and January 6, or else on January 2.[9] During the middle ages the devotion had been promoted by the Franciscans St. Bernardine of Siena and St. John of Capistrano, and in 1530 the friars were allowed to celebrate a feast of the Holy Name in mid-January. In the new Roman Missal the mass of the Holy Name is included among the votive masses. The Franciscans have kept it in their own calendar, on January 3. In the Society of Jesus the solemnity of Mary on January 1 is also celebrated as the feast of the Holy Name; some other Christian churches also celebrate the Holy Name on January 1.

The other feast of the Lord removed from the general calendar in 1969 was the feast of the Precious Blood of Jesus. It was originally proper to the Society of the Precious Blood, founded by St. Gaspar del Bufalo, and was extended to the whole church in 1849. Pope Pius X assigned it to July 1. But it seemed to duplicate the Corpus Christi observance, which is now officially the feast of the Body and Blood of Christ. The mass of the Precious Blood is still available as a votive mass.

Marian Feasts

By general agreement there were too many feasts of the Virgin Mary in the general calendar (not to mention the vast number of local festivals), but new ones continued to be added as recently as 1954. For centuries Rome had been content with the four Marian feasts of the Nativity, Annunciation, Presentation and Assumption, borrowed from the east in the seventh century. Since the Annunciation and Presentation were really feasts of the Lord, there were only two strictly Marian feasts. In the late middle ages Rome accepted the Visitation, the Conception and the Presentation of Mary. And in 1568 the local feast of the Dedication of St. Mary Major was added to the general calendar as the feast of Our Lady of the Snow.[10]

The feast of the Holy Name of Mary was instituted by Pope Innocent XI in thanksgiving for the defeat of the Turks at Vienna on September 12, 1683. (The Holy Name of Jesus was not added to the calendar until 1721.) Although it was dropped from the Roman calendar in 1969, it is still celebrated in Austria, Germany and Poland. It is also the patronal feast of Montreal, Canada.

Our Lady of Mercy (or Ransom) was the patronal feast of the Mercedarian Order founded by St. Peter Nolasco. Pope Innocent XII added it to the Roman calendar in 1696, to be celebrated on September 24. It was removed in 1969, but is still celebrated in England as the feast of Our Lady of England. Our Lady of Mercy is the patron saint of Barcelona, Spain.

Our Lady of the Rosary was another feast commemorating a victory: the naval victory over the Turks at Lepanto on October 7, 1571. It was originally celebrated in Rome as the feast of Our Lady of Victory. It was extended to the whole church in 1716 after another victory over the Turks. In the Roman calendar it is now a memorial, but the Dominican Order celebrates it as a feast.

Our Lady of Mount Carmel was the patronal feast of the Carmelite Order, celebrated on July 16. It was added to the Roman calendar in 1726. Since 1969 it has been an optional memorial.

There were formerly two feasts of Our Lady of Sorrows, a

devotion dating from the late middle ages. Pope Benedict XIII, who had added the feast of Our Lady of Mount Carmel to the general calendar in 1726, did the same for Our Lady of Sorrows in 1727. It was assigned to the Friday before Palm Sunday, and was known as the feast of the Seven Sorrows of Mary. It was removed from the calendar in 1969. The other feast was celebrated by the Servites on the Sunday after the feast of the Holy Cross (September 14). In 1814 Pope Pius VII added it to the general calendar to commemorate his return from exile after the defeat of Napoleon. In 1913 it was moved to September 15, the octave of the Nativity of Mary. In 1969 it was retained in the calendar as the memorial of Our Lady of Sorrows.

The apparition of the Virgin Mary at Lourdes in France took place on February 11, 1858. In 1907 Pope Pius X added the feast to the general calendar. However Catholics should not be required to accept a private revelation. For that reason it was made an optional memorial in 1969, and the name was changed to Our Lady of Lourdes. In France Bernadette Soubirous, who died on April 16, 1879 and was canonized in 1933, is commemorated on February 18, the octave of Our Lady of Lourdes.

The Motherhood of Mary was added to the calendar by Pope Pius XI in 1931, fifteen hundred years after the Council of Ephesus. That council had approved Mary's title of Mother of God. The feast was assigned to October 11. It was abolished in 1969, but the octave of Christmas on January 1 was given the additional title of the solemnity of Mary, Mother of God.

Devotion to the Immaculate Heart of Mary and the Sacred Heart of Jesus was promoted by St. John Eudes in the seventeenth century. In 1942 Pope Pius XII consecrated the world to the Immaculate Heart of Mary, as Leo XIII had consecrated the world to the Sacred Heart of Jesus in 1899. In 1944 the feast of the Immaculate Heart was assigned to August 22, the octave of the Assumption. Since 1969 it has been celebrated as an optional memorial on the Saturday after the feast of the Sacred Heart of Jesus. The devotion is often related to the apparition of the Virgin Mary at Fatima, Portugal in 1917. In Portugal a feast of Our Lady of Fatima is celebrated on May 13.

The feast of the Queenship of Mary was instituted by Pope Pius XII in 1954, the centenary of the dogma of the Immaculate Conception. It was assigned to May 31, the day for the feast in some local calendars since the nineteenth century. It also replaced the feast of Mary, Mediatrix of All Graces, assigned to the same day in 1918 for churches requesting it.[11] In 1969 the Queenship of Mary was reduced to a memorial and moved to August 22, the octave of the Assumption.

The appendix in the Roman Missal formerly included the following masses for local feasts of the Virgin Mary: The Marriage of Mary and Joseph (January 23), Our Lady of Good Counsel (April 26), Our Lady Help of Christians (May 24), Mary Queen of All Saints (May 31), Mary Mediatrix of All Graces (May 31), Our Lady of Grace (June 9), Our Lady of Perpetual Help (June 27), Our Lady of the Miraculous Medal (November 27), the Holy House of Loreto (December 10), Mary's Expectation of Birth (December 18), and several others. Our Lady Help of Christians is the patronal feast of Australia and New Zealand.

The great shrine of Our Lady of Guadalupe in Mexico City commemorated the apparition of Mary to the Indian Juan Diego in 1531.[12] The feast on December 12 is Mexico's patronal feast day. It was later adopted by the other countries of Latin America. In the United States it was added to the national calendar as a memorial in 1971, and raised to a feast in 1987.

Most Latin American countries also have one or more

national feasts of the Virgin Mary, such as Our Lady of Charity in Argentina, Chile and Cuba, and Our Lady of Peace in El Salvador. In Europe they include Our Lady of Czestochowa in Poland, Our Lady of Montserrat and Our Lady of the Pillar in Spain, and the Great Lady of Hungary. And in Russia the feasts of Our Lady of Kazan, Our Lady of Vladimir, and others are celebrated by the Orthodox Church.

Forces Shaping the Calendar After Trent

The additions to the Roman calendar since the Council of Trent included a number of saints of the early church overlooked during the middle ages. St. Titus, the disciple of St. Paul, was added as recently as 1854. St. Justin, author of the *Apologies* and other works, was martyred in Rome around the year 165, but was not given a feast day until 1882, along with Cyril of Alexandria and Cyril of Jerusalem. St. John of Damascus was added in 1890, St. Ephrem the Syrian in 1920, and St. Irenaeus of Lyons in 1921. And since St. Michael was the only angel mentioned by name in the old calendar, Gabriel and Raphael were given feast days in 1921.

Many of the saints added during this period were kings, queens, or royalty of some sort, reflecting the rise of nationalism in Europe. They included Emperor Henry II, Edward the Confessor of England, Margaret of Scotland, Stephen of Hungary and Elizabeth of Hungary, Wenceslaus of Bohemia, Elizabeth of Portugal, Casimir of Poland, Canute IV of Denmark, Hermenegild of Spain, and Hedwig of Silesia. They were all added to the Roman calendar between the years 1621 and 1680. On the other hand, the kings of Europe were not fond of Pope Gregory VII, who had humiliated Emperor Henry IV at Canossa in 1077. When Pope Benedict XIII dared to give St. Gregory a feast day in 1728, there was an angry reaction; in several countries the liturgical texts for the feast were banned.

The canonization of St. Robert Bellarmine, the Jesuit theologian, was delayed for the opposite reason. His views on the temporal authority of the pope were not acceptable to Sixtus V (1585–1590) and held up his canonization for centuries. Finally, in 1929, the papacy gave up its claims in exchange for the recognition of Vatican City as an independent state. Robert was canonized the following year, and was given a feast day in 1932.

Since the Roman calendar was now the general calendar for the whole western church, an effort was made to include more saints from other countries in Europe. The medieval additions to the Roman calendar were more often from the Greek church. And so St. Stanislaus of Poland was added in 1594. St. Patrick of Ireland, St. Anselm of England and St. Bridget of Sweden date from the seventeenth century. St. Isidore of Spain, St. Gertrude of Germany, and St. Rose of Lima, the first saint of the new world, were added in the eighteenth century. St. Boniface of Germany, Sts. Cyril and Methodius, the "Apostles of the Slavs," St. Augustine of Canterbury and the Venerable Bede of England were added in the period 1874–1899. St. Josaphat, archbishop of the eastern rite Catholics, was placed in the Roman calendar in 1882. The Dutch St. Peter Canisius, the French St. Theresa of the Child Jesus, and the German St. Albert the Great were added in 1926, 1927 and 1932.

But most of the saints of the Tridentine church should be identified, not with a particular country (Peter Canisius was born in the Netherlands, but worked in Germany), but with a religious order. No doubt the procedures now required for canonization favored the religious orders, since they could afford the many years, decades, or centuries of expensive litigation required to complete the process. And there were now so many religious orders, and in every one of them it was a matter of corporate pride that at least the holy founder or foundress should be commemorated in the Roman calendar. In fairness, however, most of the saintly men and women of the period were to be found precisely in those religious orders.

As the number of feast days steadily increased during this period, the number of holy days of obligation steadily decreased. The medieval holy days were literally holidays. They varied from place to place, but there were usually at least forty of them. In England the Catholics living under the penal laws had thirty-four holy days of obligation (at least in theory), reduced to eleven in 1778. The Code of Canon Law of 1917 listed ten holy days (canon 1247), and they were retained in the Code of Canon Law of 1983 (canon 1246). In the United States they were reduced to six in 1884, while France has only four. Canada recently opted for two holy days: Christmas and New Year's Day. Mexico has the same, plus Our Lady of Guadalupe. The reason given was that these were the only holy days actually observed as civil holidays.

One of the last additions to the general calendar before the reforms of the Second Vatican Council was the feast of St. Gregory Barbarigo (1625–1697). Pope John XXIII placed his name in the calendar in 1960 out of local patriotism. The pope was from Bergamo in northern Italy, and St. Gregory had been bishop of Bergamo. Pope John died in 1963, and six years later the feast of St. Gregory was dropped from the calendar.

SIX

The Second Vatican Council

Reforms Before the Council

Until the twentieth century hardly any changes were made in the Roman liturgy as reformed by the Council of Trent. In the seventeenth century Pope Urban VIII had the liturgical hymns rewritten in a style more pleasing to the classical scholars of the time.[1] But the religious orders who still had their own rites kept the original hymns, and in 1973 they were restored at last to the Latin edition of the Liturgy of the Hours. There was, of course, the ever-increasing number of new feast days and octaves. But the only serious attempt to solve that problem was made by Pope Benedict XIV in the eighteenth century, and in the end nothing was done.[2]

By the nineteenth century there were hardly any free days left in the Roman calendar, and when local feast days were added (in Europe they could be very numerous), the overcrowding was very obvious. In theory the book of Psalms was read once a week in the divine office, but in practice the same few festal psalms were repeated day after day. Finally, in 1883, Pope Leo XIII allowed the clergy to read a votive office, short, like the feast day offices, on any day not occupied by a feast. In other words, every day could now be treated as a feast day.

Then, in 1911, Pope Pius X removed one of the reasons for the excessive number of feast days by publishing a new Roman Breviary with a new arrangement of the psalms. The length of the divine office would be the same every day, whether it was a feast day or a ferial day. On most feast days the psalms and Bible readings for the weekday would be read, instead of the special festal psalms and readings, which would only be used on the major feast days. The votive offices of Pope Leo XIII were abolished.

This was only intended as a partial reform, since much more needed to be done. All the feast days were still in place. And not everyone liked the new arrangement of the psalms. The liturgical psalter had not been changed since its adoption fourteen hundred years ago.[3] At that time most of the psalms were assigned to Matins and Vespers because those were the hours of public worship. Now that the office had become the private prayer of the clergy, it seemed more convenient to move many of those psalms to the other hours of prayer. The same idea had been tried in 1535, when Cardinal Quiñonez published an experimental breviary, but then the Roman church decided to keep its ancient tradition.[4]

After 1911 nothing much happened, except for two world wars, until 1951. In that year Pope Pius XII allowed the Easter vigil to be celebrated at night, as it had been originally. For centuries it had been moved back to the morning of Holy Saturday, and in 1566 Pope Pius V had forbidden the celebration of any mass after midday, turning the custom into a law. But during the Second World War evening masses were sometimes permitted, and in 1953 a general permission was given for holy days, extended in 1957 to every day. The restored Easter vigil, with a simplified rite, was allowed as an option in 1951, but became obligatory in 1955. In that year it became part of a restored rite for all of Holy Week. Further changes were made in the Holy Week services in the Roman Missal of 1970.

In addition to the restored Holy Week services, the rubrics of the Roman Missal and Breviary were simplified in 1955. All octaves were abolished, except the octaves of Christmas, Easter and Pentecost (the octave of Pentecost was removed in 1969). So many feasts had been given octaves that they sometimes overlapped one another. Most vigils were also abolished, except for Christmas, the Ascension, Pentecost, the Assumption, St. John the Baptist, Sts. Peter and Paul, and St. Lawrence. The vigil mass was still said on the morning before the feast. (In 1969 the vigils of the Ascension and St. Lawrence were also abolished, and the others became optional masses on the evening before the feast.) The Sundays of Advent, Lent and Easter were given further protection against the intrusion of feast days.

Before the reforms of Pope Pius X, the Sunday masses were regularly displaced by the masses for saints' days. Those reforms had given the Sundays precedence over the ordinary saints' days, but not the solemnities and feasts (in modern terminology). So, for example, they still had to yield to the feasts of the apostles. By 1969, however, they could be displaced only by the feasts of the Lord and the solemnities of the Assumption, St. John the Baptist, Sts. Peter and Paul, All Saints, and the patronal festival. The Immaculate Conception, which still had precedence over the Advent Sundays in 1955, had to yield to those Sundays in 1969.

In the same way the Lenten weekday masses were gradually restored. At first they had to yield to every saint's day. Then they could be said instead of the mass of the saint, at the choice of the priest. By 1969 they had precedence over the saint's day, and most of the saints had been removed from the Lenten season anyway.

Pope Pius XII died in 1958 and was succeeded by Pope John XXIII. In 1960 the classification of feast days into different kinds of "doubles" and "simples" (semidoubles had been eliminated in 1955) was changed to feasts of the first, second and third class, and commemorations. However the new system was not well received: most of the saints were in the third class, and the church seemed to be calling them third-class saints. In 1969 a more traditional system of solemnities, feasts, and memorials was adopted.

In the reforms of 1960 a few feast days were given a higher rank, and ten were reduced to commemorations. The new commemorations included Our Lady of Mount Carmel and Our Lady of Mercy, St. George and St. Alexis, St. Eustace and St. Cyriacus. In the case of the four saints, the change was a tactful way of getting rid of their fictional legends, since the Roman Breviary did not have a biographical reading on a commemoration, only on a feast day.

Also, for the first time since 1568, nine feast days were actually removed from the calendar. However they were all duplicates of feast days assigned to other days, e.g. the second feast of St. Peter's Chair, the second feast of the Holy Cross, St. Anacletus (who was the same person as St. Cletus), and secondary feasts of St. Michael, St. John the Apostle, St. Stephen, etc.

A more drastic reform was carried out in the appendix of the Roman Missal for local feast days. Sixteen of the masses were removed, since they really belonged in the supplements of the Roman Missal for particular countries or dioceses or churches. They included the Holy House of Loreto, the Marriage of Mary and Joseph, Mary's Expectation of Birth, and votive masses for the Fridays of Lent in honor of the Crown of Thorns, the Holy Shroud, the Five Wounds, etc. The mass of St. John of Nepomuc was removed because it was based on the legend that he died rather than reveal the secrets of confession (he was venerated as the patron saint of Bohemia).

The mass of St. Philomena was not only removed from the appendix of the Roman Missal; it was even removed from local calendars ("e quolibet calendario expungendae") and abolished entirely.[5] In 1802 some human remains were found in the catacomb of St. Priscilla. It was believed at the time that it was the body of a virgin-martyr named Philomena. She was enshrined in the church in Mugnano del Cardinale near Naples, where the parish priest produced a life of the saint. Miracles were reported, and in 1837 the diocese of Nola was allowed to celebrate her feast day on August 11. A proper mass and office was approved in 1855. But further investigation, dating from 1904, cast doubt on the whole story and led to her removal from the calendar.[6]

Vatican II

Pope John XXIII opened the Second Vatican Council in 1962, but he died the following year, before the publication of the Constitution on the Sacred Liturgy in December of 1963. The council called for a general restoration of the liturgy, giving special attention to the liturgical year.[7] Sunday, "the foundation and kernel of the whole liturgical year," should have precedence over other celebrations. The feasts of the Lord in the Proper of the Time should be given due preference over the feasts of the saints. And only saints of universal importance should be commemorated in the general calendar. The reformed Roman calendar was published by Pope Paul VI in 1969.[8] The reformed Roman Missal, Liturgy of the Hours (Divine Office), and other liturgical books followed, in Latin and in vernacular editions.

These reforms brought to a successful conclusion the work of the liturgical movement begun by Prosper Guéranger (1805–1875), the abbot of Solesmes in France. It was carried on by the abbeys of Mont-César and Saint-André (the St. Andrew's Missal) in Belgium, Maria Laach in Germany (Ildefons Herwegen and Odo Casel), Klosterneuburg in Austria (Pius Parsch), St. John's in Minnesota (Virgil Michel), and many other communities and individuals, Protestant, Catholic, and Eastern Orthodox.

The liturgical year now has only the four seasons of Advent, Christmas, Lent and Easter, plus "Ordinary Time." The elimination of Septuagesima and Passiontide was approved by other Christian churches, but some preferred to keep the traditional Sundays after Epiphany and Pentecost (or Trinity). The Easter season ends on Pentecost Sunday, which lost its octave. However in countries where the following day (Whitmonday) is a holiday, the mass of Pentecost or the votive mass of the Holy Spirit can be celebrated.

In countries where the Epiphany, the Ascension, and Corpus Christi are not holy days of obligation, they are transferred to the following Sunday (or the nearest Sunday in the case of the Epiphany). These changes have created some tensions. While it probably doesn't matter whether Corpus Christi is celebrated on Thursday or Sunday, some have called for the observance of the Epiphany and the Ascension on the proper days. Also, the Christmas-Epiphany season is complicated enough with the fixed holy days falling on different days of the week without adding the further complication of two different ways of celebrating the Epiphany. In some years the Epiphany falls on the same Sunday as the feast of the Baptism of the Lord, in which case the latter is moved to Monday.

The feasts of the Lord include several devotional feasts which have been retained in the reformed calendar: the Holy Trinity, Corpus Christi, the Sacred Heart, and Christ the King, and also the Holy Family. The feasts of the Holy Name and the Precious Blood were dropped, but they can still be celebrated as votive masses. Corpus Christi is now officially known as the solemnity of the Body and Blood of Christ.

Most of the feasts of the Virgin Mary were kept in the calendar, but four of them were reduced to memorials (the Queenship of Mary, Our Lady of Sorrows, Our Lady of the Rosary, and the Presentation of Mary) and four more were reduced to optional memorials (Our Lady of Lourdes, the

Immaculate Heart, Our Lady of Mount Carmel, and the Dedication of St. Mary Major). The Holy Name of Mary and Our Lady of Mercy were left for local calendars.

Because of its apocryphal background there was some surprise that the Presentation of Mary was kept, but it is an important day in many religious orders. On the other hand, the Queenship of Mary (an awkward title) is already celebrated on the feast of the Assumption, and only dates from 1954. The Maternity of Mary, formerly on October 11, was assigned to January 1, the octave of Christmas, which already had a certain Marian emphasis. The parents of Mary, "Joachim and Ann," who formerly had separate feast days, now have a common memorial on July 26.

As decreed by the Second Vatican Council, only saints "of universal importance" should be kept in the general calendar. That was certainly the most difficult task of the committee charged with revising the calendar. The Tridentine reform of 1568 was a much simpler matter: they went back to the ancient calendar of the city of Rome, which was mainly a list of Roman martyrs, to which they added a few medieval saints. The procedure followed in 1969 was just the opposite: most of the Roman martyrs were discarded. They kept only four obligatory memorials: St. Agnes, St. Justin, Sts. Cornelius and Cyprian, and St. Ignatius of Antioch (who died in Rome). St. Lawrence, the Roman deacon and martyr, had the distinction of being the only non-biblical saint to be honored with a "feast" rather than a simple "memorial." Nine others, including five popes, were listed as optional memorials. They also added a new optional memorial in memory of the First Martyrs of Rome, under the emperor Nero, on June 30, following the feast of Sts. Peter and Paul.

The saints created out of the names of the Roman *tituli,* or parish churches, were all dropped from the calendar except for St. Cecilia. She was kept "because of popular devotion," and was even given an obligatory memorial. Also dropped were all the other saints who "pose serious historical problems." There were twenty-nine saints in that category, saints who had been very popular in the middle ages, such as St. Alexis, St. Margaret, St. Eustace, St. Ursula, St. Catherine of Alexandria, St. Barbara, and St. Christopher. Even in 1969 there were loud protests about St. Christopher, although few of the protesters could remember the date of his feast day. (He never had a feast day, only a commemoration on the feast of St. James the Apostle on July 25.) The church in Germany, however, was kind enough to keep several of these saints in the national calendar: St. Margaret, St. Ursula, St. Catherine, St. Barbara, and St. Christopher.

There were no less than thirty-eight popes in the general calendar (and even more in the diocese of Rome), thanks to Pope Gregory VII (1073–1085), who thought that all popes should be honored as saints. Only fifteen were kept in the new calendar. There were six martyrs of the early church and two later martyrs, plus St. Sylvester and St. Damasus, St. Leo the Great and St. Gregory the Great, St. Gregory VII, St. Pius V, and St. Pius X.

That left a great many other saints from many countries and all centuries. The martyrs were given preference, according to tradition. Then came the various national saints, the founders of the more important religious orders, and all the doctors of the church. To give the calendar a better geographical balance, many of the Italian saints were dropped and some new memorials were added: Sts. John Fisher and Thomas More of England, St. Columban of Ireland, St. Ansgar for Scandinavia, the Japanese Martyrs, the Martyrs of Uganda, the North American Martyrs, St. Turibius and St. Martin de Porres of Lima, and St. Peter Chanel for Oceania.

There was also a new Italian saint: Maria Goretti. In 1902 the twelve year old girl was killed during a rape attempt. Miracles were reported through her intercession, and she was canonized in 1950 as a martyr. Although she did not die for the Christian faith, she did die in defense of Christian virtue. Her case has been described as "unique in hagiology."[9]

The Roman Calendar Today

The results of the calendar reform were as follows. The ten solemnities included only biblical saints: the Virgin Mary, St. Joseph, St. John the Baptist, and Sts. Peter and Paul (plus All Saints Day). The twenty-three "feasts" were also limited to biblical saints with the exception of St. Lawrence. The feast of St. Michael the Archangel had been raised to a double of the first class (a solemnity in modern terminology) in 1917, but it was now included among the feasts. Therefore all the other saints were now found among the sixty-three memorials and the ninety-five optional memorials. In 1979, shortly after the election of Pope John Paul II, the optional memorial of St. Stanislaus was made obligatory, and the obligatory memorial of St. Maximilian Kolbe was added in 1983. The Korean Martyrs were given a memorial in 1985, St. Lawrence Ruiz (the first Filipino saint) and Companions in 1988, and the Martyrs of Vietnam in 1989.

Many of the memorials were assigned to new dates, usually the date of death. In the old calendar they were often put on some other day, either through error or because the date of death was occupied by another feast day. It was also possible to celebrate the feast of one saint with a commemoration of another. But the new calendar allows only one feast or obligatory memorial on a given day. There can be two or more *optional* memorials on the same day, but in that case only one can be celebrated.

Some countries have chosen different dates. They often decided to keep the old dates because the people preferred them. The German calendar, for example, kept the old dates for St. Matthias the Apostle, the Visitation, St. Gertrude, St. Elizabeth, and St. Peter Canisius. In Poland the feast of St. Stanislaus is celebrated on May 8, not on April 11. In Hungary the feast of St. Stephen is on August 20, not August 16. In the Czech and Slovak churches Sts. Cyril and Methodius are commemorated on July 5, not February 14.

Several feast days were moved in 1969 to avoid the Lenten or Advent seasons. St. Thomas Aquinas, who died on March 7, was moved to January 28, the day of his Translation. St. Gregory the Great, who died on March 12, was moved to September 3, the day of his ordination as bishop of Rome. And St. Benedict was moved from his principal feast day on March 21 to another traditional feast day on July 11.

Even some apostles were given new dates. St. Thomas was moved to July 3, his feast day in the Syrian church, because December 21, the old day, was too close to Christmas. The feast of St. Matthias on February 24 often fell in Lent, but in his case there was no obvious alternative date. May 14 was chosen because it is in the Easter season, and Matthias became an apostle soon after the ascension. Sts. Philip and James were displaced by St. Joseph the Worker on May 1, and are now on May 3. All these changes have caused some confusion, not only in the Catholic Church but also in other communions, especially the Lutheran and Anglican. In most cases, however, the new dates are obviously better. St. Margaret of Scotland, for example, has been restored to November 16, the anniversary of her death (the old date was June 10).

National and Religious Calendars

A reform along the same lines was also required in the calendars of every country and religious order. But the new rules made that more difficult than it had been in the past.

Formerly local feast days had precedence, as a rule, over feasts in the Roman calendar, and both could be celebrated on the same day. In England, for example, May 26 was the feast of St. Augustine of Canterbury, with a commemoration of the Roman feast of St. Philip Neri. Now, however, the Roman feast days had precedence, and only one feast or obligatory memorial was allowed on a given day. And so, even in England, May 26 was now the memorial of St. Philip, and the feast of St. Augustine was moved to the following day. In Ireland June 3 was the feast of St. Kevin, the patron saint of Dublin. But June 3 was now the memorial of the Uganda Martyrs, and so St. Kevin was moved to June 4.

Actually the Roman authorities probably did not expect such strict obedience to their rules, which were intended to keep the saints' days on the same day everywhere, as far as possible. Exceptions "for pastoral reasons" were allowed, and probably expected.[10] There was also a rule that only the more important saints should be included in the calendar of a country, or diocese, or religious order, and the rest should be venerated locally.[11] This rule was also interpreted more strictly in some places than in others. In Ireland the national calendar was reduced from sixty-five saints' days to only five: St. Brigid, St. Patrick, St. Columba, St. Columban, and All Saints of Ireland.[12] On the other hand, there are about seventy entries in the present German regional calendar.

Among the religious orders, the Franciscans led all the rest in the number of saints' days. They had so many, in fact, that in 1950 they began bunching them together in groups of three to relieve the overcrowding. Therefore the approximately eighty entries in their present calendar (including some proper to the Second and Third Orders) can be considered modest by comparison.[13] The Dominicans, with about thirty feasts and memorials, are more typical of the principal religious orders in the church.

The churches of the new world had just the opposite problem: too few saints of their own. The United States finally acquired a feast day in 1930, when the North American Martyrs were canonized. Since they were French Jesuits, they are venerated in Canada as the Canadian Martyrs. Then Mother Cabrini was canonized in 1946, Mother Seton in 1975, and Bishop Neumann of Philadelphia in 1977. Mother Duchesne of the Society of the Sacred Heart was canonized in 1988, and several others have been beatified: Mother Drexel, Father Serra, and (jointly with Canada) Kateri Tekakwitha, Brother André, and Mother Durocher.[14] In Canada Mother Marguerite Bourgeoys was canonized in 1982, and others have been beatified: Marie of the Incarnation, Bishop Laval of Quebec, and Marguerite d'Youville. In Latin America, although St. Rose of Lima was the first saint of the new world to be canonized (in 1671), there have been very few canonizations since then.[15]

The Lutheran and Anglican churches, meanwhile, have added many non-biblical saints to their liturgical calendars. When compared with the simplified Catholic calendar, the result has been "a notable convergence of approach in the three churches."[16] In the United States the Lutheran calendar now has about one hundred and twenty-five entries, and the Episcopal calendar about one hundred and fifty.[17] In addition to the feasts of the Lord, the apostles, etc., they all have a feast of the Virgin Mary on August 15 and St. Joseph on March 19. For the later saints, before the reformation, the selections are very similar. For the modern period, the memorials reflect the different traditions of the three communions, although the Lutheran calendar is quite ecumenical. It includes St. Francis Xavier, St. John of the Cross, St. Teresa of Avila, and Pope John XXIII.

SEVEN

Unfinished Business

The Date of Easter

At the end of the Constitution on the Sacred Liturgy of the Second Vatican Council there is a short appendix. The council declared that it was not opposed to the idea of assigning Easter to a fixed Sunday and the idea of a perpetual calendar. In regard to the date of Easter, the Council of Nicaea in 325 decided that it should be celebrated on the Sunday after the first full moon after the spring equinox. Earlier, in the second century, the churches of Asia Minor celebrated the paschal feast on the same day as the Jewish Passover, on the day of the full moon, or 14 Nisan in the Jewish calendar (hence the "Quartodeciman controversy"). But the other churches, notably the Roman church, insisted on commemorating the resurrection on a Sunday. In theory Easter Sunday should always be the Sunday after the Jewish Passover, but because of different methods of computation, that is not always the case. Obviously there was nothing sacred about the date of Easter, but it did seem proper that all the churches should celebrate the festival on the same day.

The spring equinox, which determined the date of Easter, was fixed on March 21 in the Julian calendar used in the Roman empire. The Julian calendar was reasonably accurate. There were three hundred and sixty-five days in the year, and an extra day every four years. That was only eleven minutes too long, but by the sixteenth century that amounted to an error of ten days. The real spring equinox was on March 11 instead of March 21. The church had been aware of the problem for some time, since reports had been sent to the Council of Constance (1414–1418), the Council of Basle (1431–1437), and the Council of Trent (1545–1563). Pope Pius V was responsible for the liturgical reforms of the Council of Trent, but the calendar problem was left to his successor, Gregory XIII (1572–1585).

The obvious solution was to reduce the number of leap years. After consulting the astronomers, including the Jesuit Christopher Clavius, in 1582 the pope decided to make the centennial years leap years only if they were exactly divisible by 400. The year 1600 would be a leap year, and the year 2000, but not 1700, 1800 or 1900. Secondly, to bring the equinox back to March 21, he dropped ten days from the calendar. The day after the feast of St. Francis would be October 15, not October 5.

The Gregorian calendar was accepted by the Catholic countries, but the Protestant states did not want to give the impression that they were taking orders from the pope. In 1700, after waiting for more than a hundred years, the Protestant parts of Germany accepted the reform, along with Denmark and the Netherlands. The British, and the American colonies, accepted the "new style" in 1752, and Sweden a year later. No progress was made during the nineteenth century, except for Japan in 1873. China followed in 1912. The Russian Orthodox Church clung to the Julian calendar, but after the October Revolution in 1917 (which was really in November), the new communist government of the Soviet Union changed to the Gregorian calendar. Finally, in 1923, the Greek church and government also changed over, but the Russian church continued to follow the Julian calendar.

A more radical reform had been attempted after the French Revolution, as part of the anti-Christian campaign. The year 1792 became the Year One of the new era. Every month had thirty days, with five extra days at the end of the year in September. The months were given new names, and were divided into three decades instead of four weeks, so that the day of rest was on the tenth day rather than the seventh. But after thirteen years, it was abandoned in 1806.

The Gregorian calendar caused difficulties, first between the Catholic and Orthodox churches, and after 1923 between the Orthodox churches that accepted it and those that did not. By the twentieth century the Julian calendar had fallen thirteen days behind the Gregorian, so that Christmas, for example, fell on January 7. Easter, as a movable feast, was not affected directly, but it had to come after the spring equinox, which was on April 3 instead of March 21. If the full moon was early, the Orthodox Easter would be postponed to the next full moon. If the full moon was later, the Orthodox would celebrate Easter with the rest of the church.[1] There was also a "calendar problem" among the Eastern Catholic churches.[2]

The question discussed at the Second Vatican Council was whether the Christian churches might agree to celebrate Easter on a fixed Sunday, not determined by the age of the moon. At present, Easter can fall on any day between March 22 and April 25, a variation that also affects all the other movable feasts, including Ash Wednesday, Palm Sunday, Good Friday, Ascension Day, Pentecost, Trinity Sunday, Corpus Christi, and the Sacred Heart. In the sixteenth century the Jesuit astronomer Clavius favored the idea of a fixed Sunday for Easter.[3] Martin Luther also complained about the "wobbling festivals."[4] Recent proposals would assign Easter to the second Sunday in April, which was probably on or close to the actual date of the resurrection.[5] But the council was not willing to make such a change without the consent of the other Christian churches.

A Perpetual Calendar

The council also considered the possibility of a perpetual calendar. Actually the calendar used in the Roman empire *was* a perpetual calendar until the emperor Constantine adopted the Judaeo-Christian week in the year 321. Fifty-two weeks are one day short of a full year (two days in leap year), and so every year the holidays and holy days fall on different days of the week. That is not a major inconvenience, but it could be remedied, and at the same time the calendar could be put into a more logical order. Combined with a fixed Sunday for Easter, the problem of calculating the date of Easter could be solved once and for all.

The "World Calendar" was first proposed by an Italian priest, Marco Mastrofini, in 1834. The last day of the year would be detached from the week, or the last two days in leap year. In that way every year could begin on a Sunday, and all the holidays would fall on the same day of the week every year. Later developments of the plan evened out the months by giving thirty-one days to the first month in each quarter, and thirty days to the other months. The months with thirty-one days would have five Sundays instead of four, and so the number of weekdays in every month would be the same. It was also proposed that the extra day in a leap year be added to the month of June.[6]

A rival plan, known as the "International Fixed Calendar," achieved even greater uniformity by dividing the year into thirteen months of twenty-eight days each, plus the extra day. But there was not much interest in a plan that would abandon the twelve-month year, so easily divided into quarters. Even the World Calendar ran into opposition from some religious communities, mainly Jews, Muslims and fundamentalist Christians, who believed that the succession of weeks should never be broken. To accommodate them the Vatican Council declared that the succession of weeks should be left intact, unless there are "extremely weighty reasons to the contrary."

That could be done by omitting the extra day (or two days in leap year), and letting them add up to a full week, which could then be attached to that year. A year would then have either three hundred and sixty-four days or three hundred and seventy-one days. But in that case the equinoxes and solstices would not fall on the same days every year, and there would be even less uniformity than there is now. Furthermore the year is the natural unit of time, while the week is an artificial arrangement that could still serve its purpose if an extra day were added once a year. The sabbath was made for man, not man for the sabbath.

Notes

1. The Early Christian Church

1. *Didache,* 14.
2. Ignatius of Antioch, Magnesians, 9.
3. Letter of Barnabas, 15.9.
4. Pliny the Younger, Epp. X.96. The text is available in Kirch, *Enchiridion Fontium Historiae Ecclesiasticae Antiquae* (Barcelona, 1965), p. 22. English translation in Bettenson, *Documents of the Christian Church* (Oxford, 1947), p. 5.
5. Justin Martyr, *Apology,* I.65–67.
6. *Ibid.,* 67.
7. Justin Martyr, *Dialogue with Trypho,* 10.
8. *Ibid.,* 41.
9. *Didache,* 8.
10. Cf. also 1 Pet 1:19 and Rev 5:12 and passim.
11. Eusebius, *Church History,* 5.23–25.
12. Melito of Sardis, *Paschal Homily.* English translation in A. Hamman, *The Paschal Mystery* (Staten Island, 1969), 26–39.
13. Second Vatican Council, Constitution on the Sacred Liturgy, 102. English translation in Austin Flannery, *Vatican Council II* (Northport, 1984), p. 29.
14. Cf. Adolf Adam, *The Liturgical Year* (New York, 1981), p. 62.
15. Bede, *De temporum ratione,* 1.15.
16. Bede, *Ecclesiastical History,* 3.25; 5.15,22.

17. Tertullian, *De baptismo* (On Baptism), 19.
18. Hippolytus, *Apostolic Tradition*. English translation by Gregory Dix, reissued by Henry Chadwick (London, 1968), chapter 20. French translation by Bernard Botte (Sources chrétiennes, 11), chapter 20. Hippolytus does associate Easter with baptism in his *Commentary on Daniel,* 1.16 (Sources chrétiennes, 14), p. 84. Cf. Thomas J. Talley, *The Origins of the Liturgical Year* (New York, 1986), p. 35.
19. Cf. Talley, *Origins,* p. 195.
20. *The Martyrdom of Polycarp.* Text and translation in Kirsopp Lake, *The Apostolic Fathers* (Loeb Classical Library), II, 307–345. Cf. chapters 16–18.
21. Tertullian, *De oratione* (On Prayer), 23.
22. *Ibid.,* 25. Morning and evening prayers were the *legitimae orationes.*
23. Tertullian, *De jejunio* (On Fasting), 10.
24. Tertullian, *De oratione,* 25; Origen, *De oratione,* 12.
25. *Apostolic Tradition,* chapter 36 in Dix, chapter 41 in Botte.
26. Origen, *De oratione,* 12.
27. In later centuries monasteries would often schedule the night office for cockcrow rather than midnight.
28. Cyprian, *De dominica oratione* (On the Lord's Prayer), 36.
29. *Apostolic Tradition,* chapter 35 in Dix, chapter 41 in Botte.
30. In the early monasteries (and even today in the east), the Bible was read privately, not in the Liturgy of the Hours. Cf. A.G. Martimort, *The Church at Prayer* (Collegeville, 1986), IV, 220.
31. *Apostolic Tradition,* chapter 26 in Dix, chapter 25 in Botte.
32. A. Baumstark, *Comparative Liturgy* (Westminster,

1958), pp. 15–30. Summarized in H. Wegman, *Christian Worship in East and West* (New York, 1985), p. xiv.

33. Baumstark, *Liturgy,* p. 59. His ideas about the influence of the Bible on the liturgy were slightly modified by Bernard Botte, who revised the text, on p. 59, note 2.

2. The Christian Roman Empire

1. Gregory Dix, *The Shape of the Liturgy* (Westminster, 1945), pp. 333–360.
2. Cf. Thomas J. Talley, "History and Eschatology in the Primitive Pascha," *Worship* 47 (1973), pp. 212–221.
3. Cf. Robert Taft, "Historicism Revisted," *Beyond East and West* (Washington, D.C., 1984), p. 16.
4. Text in Kirch, *Enchiridion Fontium Historiae Ecclesiasticae Antiquae* (Barcelona, 1965), pp. 331–332.
5. St. Augustine, Sermon 202. Cf. Hans Lietzmann, *A History of the Early Church* (London, 1961), III, 317.
6. Text in Bettenson, *Documents of the Christian Church* (Oxford, 1947), p. 27.
7. Cf. Hippolytus, *On the Antichrist,* 61; Cyprian, *On the Lord's Prayer,* 35.
8. *De pascha computus,* 19 (CSEL 3.3, 266).
9. Hippolytus, *Commentary on Daniel,* IV, 23 (SC 14, 187).
10. Cf. Louis Duchesne, *Christian Worship* (London, 1919), p. 258; J. Quasten, *Patrology* II (Westminster, 1953), p. 172.
11. Duchesne, *Christian Worship,* pp. 261–265.
12. Cf. Thomas J. Talley, *The Origins of the Liturgical Year* (New York, 1986), pp. 91–99.
13. Sozomen, *Church History,* VII, 18.
14. Talley, *Origins,* pp. 8–9.
15. Clement, *Stromata,* I, 21, 146.

16. John Wilkinson, trans., *Egeria's Travels to the Holy Land* (Jerusalem, 1981). Egeria is also the name used in *Ancient Christian Writers,* Vol. 38. The *Oxford Dictionary of the Christian Church* calls her Etheria. The *New Catholic Encyclopedia* (11, 119) calls her Aetheria.

17. Eusebius, *Life of Constantine,* III, 25–40 (NPNF, Second Series, I, 526–530).

18. Cf. Cyril E. Pocknee, *The Christian Altar* (London, 1963), pp. 88–100. The Church of the Holy Sepulcher was reconstructed in the twelfth century with the altar at the east end.

19. Cf. Wilkinson, "The Old Armenian Lectionary," in *Travels,* pp. 253–277. The readings for the other days of Holy Week are also found in the Armenian Lectionary.

20. The newly-baptized were brought into the church during the song of the three young men, at the end of the last reading.

21. Cf. Talley, *Origins,* pp. 47–54.

22. Cf. Talley, *Origins,* p. 64.

23. The Maccabees were only given a commemoration, not a feast, on August 1, but a commemoration of one saint is no longer allowed on the feast of another saint.

24. St. Gregory of Nyssa, *Oratio funebris in laudem Basilii* (PG 46, 789). Cf. Duchesne, *Christian Worship,* pp. 265B–268.

25. St. Cyril, *Letter to Constantius* (PG 33, 1165–1179).

26. Cf. Daniel Wm. O'Connor, *Peter in Rome* (New York, 1969), pp. 116–134.

27. Cf. A.G. Martimort, *The Church at Prayer* (Collegeville, 1986), IV, 109.

28. Cf. Duchesne, *Christian Worship,* pp. 277–280.

29. Text in DACL 8/1, 635 (with many misspellings).

30. Cf. Peter Llewellyn, *Rome in the Dark Ages* (New York, 1971), pp. 173–198.

31. Cf. Walter Howard Frere, *Studies in Early Roman Liturgy,* I. *The Kalendar* (Alcuin Club Coll. xxviii), p. 27.
32. St. Paulinus, *Vita Ambrosii,* 14; St. Ambrose, Epistle 22; St. Augustine, *Confessions,* IX, 7.
33. St. Paulinus, *Vita Ambrosii,* 32–33.
34. St. Basil, Epistle 197.
35. Cod. Theod. IX, xvii, 7 (26 Feb. 386): "Humatum corpus nemo ad alterum locum transferat; nemo martyrem distrahat, nemo mercetur."
36. Cf. Frere, *Studies,* pp. 140–141.
37. Tertullian, *De praescriptione,* 36.
38. *Didascalia Apostolorum,* V, 18 (ANF VII, 447), Cf. Talley, *Origins,* pp. 27–31.
39. Text in Alberigo, *Conciliorum Oecumenicorum Decreta* (Bologna, 1973), p. 8.
40. *Apostolic Constitutions,* VIII, 47, canon 37 (or 38) (ANF VII, 502). Cf. Talley, *Origins,* p. 63.
41. St. Athanasius, Festal Letters (NPNF, Second Series, IV, 512).
42. St. Athanasius, Festal Letters (NPNF, Second Series, IV, 538).
43. Cf. Baumstark, *Comparative Liturgy,* p. 194; Talley, *Origins,* pp. 189–194.
44. Socrates, *Church History,* V, 22 (NPNF, Second Series, II, 131).
45. *Apostolic Constitutions,* V, 13 (ANF VII, 443).
46. Pope Innocent I, Epistle 25, 10 (PL 20, 559).
47. Pope Leo I, Sermon 19, 2 (PL 54, 186).
48. Pope Leo I, Sermon 12, 4 (PL 54, 171). For Pope Gelasius on ordinations: PL 59, 158.
49. Gregory of Tours, *History of the Franks,* II, 34 (PL 71, 231).
50. Gregory of Tours, *History of the Franks,* X, 31 (PL 71, 566).

51. Cf. Adolf Adam, *The Liturgical Year* (New York, 1981), p. 131.
52. Egeria, *Travels,* 48.1–3.

3. The Early Middle Ages

1. In 1934 Pope Pius XI made two additions to the list of stational churches: St. Agatha as an alternative to St. Pudentiana, and St. Frances of Rome (also known as Santa Maria Nuova) as an alternative to St. Apollinaris.
2. April 28 was the dedication day of the church of St. Vitalis in Rome.
3. Cf. Egeria, *Travels,* 25, 6–10. In Jerusalem the birth of Christ was celebrated on the Epiphany, January 6.
4. Cf. Herman Wegman, *Christian Worship in East and West* (New York, 1985), pp. 151–164.
5. Cf. Baumstark, *Comparative Liturgy,* pp. 97–102.
6. Cf. Martimort, *The Church at Prayer,* IV, 68–69.
7. *Ibid.,* p. 71.
8. *Ibid.,* pp. 49–50.
9. Cf. Archdale A. King, *The Liturgy of the Roman Church* (Milwaukee, 1957), p. 193.
10. Cf. Egeria, *Travels,* 35, 1–2.
11. Cf. Martimort, *The Church at Prayer,* IV, 47–49.
12. E.g., Ludwig Eisenhofer and Joseph Lechner, *The Liturgy of the Roman Rite* (New York, 1961), p. 190.
13. Cf. Martimort, *The Church at Prayer,* IV, 37.
14. Code of Canon Law (1917), canon 1252, 2.
15. Cf. *Apostolic Constitutions,* V, 20, 14 (ANF VII, 449).
16. Cf. William R. Bonniwell, O.P., *A History of the Dominican Liturgy* (New York, 1944), p. 176.
17. Cf. Egeria, *Travels,* 48, 1.
18. St. Ambrose, *Sermon on the Death of Theodosius,* 46 (PL

16, 1399). Cf. Wilkinson, *Egeria's Travels,* Note C, pp. 240–241.

19. Cf. Wilkinson, *Egeria's Travels,* p. 274, note 64.
20. *Protoevangelium of James,* 17. Cf. Hennecke-Schnee-melcher, *New Testament Apocrypha* (Philadelphia, 1963), I, 383.
21. *Protoevangelium of James,* 7.
22. Bernard Botte, "La première fête mariale de la liturgie romaine," EL 47 (1933), 425–430.
23. Cf. Martimort, *The Church at Prayer,* IV, 132–138.
24. The Council in Trullo, canon 52 (NPNF, 2nd Series, XIV, 389).
25. The Donation of Constantine in Sidney Z. Ehler and John B. Morrall, *Church and State Through the Centuries* (Westminster, 1954), pp. 15–22.
26. Cf. Frere, *The Kalendar,* p. 115.
27. Cf. J.B. O'Connell, *The Roman Martyrology* (Westminster, 1962), p. 191.
28. Cf. Archdale A. King, *The Liturgies of the Past* (Milwaukee, 1959), p. 60.
29. Cf. Frere, *The Kalendar,* p. 138.
30. Code of Canon Law (1917), canon 806, 1.
31. In the Byzantine tradition Saturdays are dedicated to all saints and all souls.
32. Gregory of Tours, *History of the Franks,* I, 30.
33. *Dictatus papae* in Ehler-Morrall, *Church and State,* p. 44.
34. Tertullian rejected the Acts of Paul and Thecla as fictional in *De baptismo,* 17 (ANF III, 677).

4. The Later Middle Ages

1. Noële M. Denis-Boulet, *The Christian Calendar* (New York, 1960), p. 93.

2. Martimort, *The Church at Prayer,* IV, 120–123. The text of Ado's martyrology is in PL 123: 143–178.

3. Cf. Louise Ropes Loomis, *The Book of the Popes* (New York, 1916).

4. He is still commemorated in the Benedictine calendar as Celestine V, pope and hermit.

5. Cf. Thurston-Attwater, *Butler's Lives of the Saints,* I, 188–189.

6. Cf. "Canonizzazione," in *Enciclopedia Cattolica,* III, 569–607.

7. Cf. Archdale A. King, *Liturgies of the Religious Orders* (Milwaukee, 1955).

8. Cf. S.J.P. van Dijk and J. Hazelden Walker, *The Origins of the Modern Roman Liturgy* (London, 1960), pp. 423–447.

9. Cf. William R. Bonniwell, O.P., *A History of the Dominican Liturgy* (New York, 1944), pp. 98–117.

10. *Ibid.,* pp. 344–345.

11. *Ibid.,* pp. 275–279.

12. Bernold of Constance, *Micrologus,* 60 (PL 151: 1019–1020).

13. In many churches the preface of the Trinity was said at mass on Sundays from the thirteenth century, but was not authorized by Rome until 1759.

14. Martimort, *The Church at Prayer,* IV, 104, note 23.

15. *Ibid.,* p. 140, note 26.

16. Adolf Adam, *The Liturgical Year* (New York, 1981), p. 222, note 37.

17. Martimort, *The Church at Prayer,* IV, 97–98.

18. *Ibid.,* pp. 139–140.

19. Erasmus, *The Praise of Folly,* 40. According to the commentary in the *Calendarium Romanum* (Vatican City, 1969), p. 131, the commemoration of St. Christopher

dates from around 1550. But it seems to have been in the Roman calendar in the thirteenth century: cf. Van Dijk and Walker, *The Origins of the Modern Roman Liturgy* (London, 1960), pp. 436–437.

5. The Reformation and the Council of Trent

1. John Calvin, *Institutes of the Christian Religion,* III, 20, 21–27.
2. H.J. Schroeder, O.P., *The Canons and Decrees of the Council of Trent* (Rockford, 1978 reprint of 1941 ed.), p. 216.
3. Cf. Theodor Klauser, *A Short History of the Western Liturgy,* 2nd edition (Oxford, 1979), pp. 124–129.
4. Comparative table in *Catholic Encyclopedia* (New York, 1913), III, 165; reproduced in Noële M. Denis-Boulet, *The Christian Calendar* (New York, 1960), p. 104.
5. The feast days still in the Roman calendar are given their present dates, which often differ from the original dates.
6. Cf. Martimort, *The Church at Prayer,* IV, 105–106.
7. *Ibid.,* pp. 106–107.
8. Quoted in Adolf Adam, *The Liturgical Year* (New York, 1981), p. 178.
9. Before 1913 the Holy Name was celebrated on the second Sunday after Epiphany.
10. According to legend, the site for the church was designated by a miraculous August snowfall.
11. Belgium kept the feast of Mary Mediatrix, moving it to August 31. In some religious orders it was moved to May 8.
12. Juan Diego was beatified in 1990; his memorial in Mexico is on December 9.

6. The Second Vatican Council

1. Cf. Pierre Batiffol, *History of the Roman Breviary* (London, 1898), pp. 281–288. For the original hymns: Aquinas Byrnes, *The Hymns of the Dominican Missal and Breviary* (St. Louis, 1943). For the revised hymns: Dom Matthew Britt, *The Hymns of the Breviary and Missal* (New York, 1952).
2. Batiffol, *History,* pp. 289–350.
3. Cf. John Alexander Lamb, *The Psalms in Christian Worship* (London, 1962), pp. 112–115.
4. J. Wickham Legg, ed., *Breviarium Romanum a Francisco Cardinali Quignonio* (Cambridge, 1888; reprint 1970).
5. Cf. *Ephemerides Liturgicae* 75 (1961), p. 424, note 22.
6. Cf. AAS 53 (1961), p. 174. Thurston-Attwater, *Butler's Lives of the Saints,* III, 299–301.
7. Constitution on the Sacred Liturgy, Chapter V (102–111), in Austin Flannery, ed., *Vatican Council II,* revised ed. (Northport, 1984), I, 28–31.
8. *Calendarium Romanum* (Vatican City, 1969). English text in U.S. Catholic Conference, *Norms Governing Liturgical Calendars* (Washington, D.C., 1984).
9. Thurston-Attwater, *Butler's Lives of the Saints,* III, 28–29.
10. U.S. Catholic Conference, *Norms,* Part One, 56d (p. 22); Part Two, 23c (p. 45).
11. *Ibid.,* Part Two, 17 (p. 44).
12. Oliver Plunkett, archbishop of Armagh and martyr, was added to the national calendar after his canonization in 1975. Cf. Mary Ryan D'Arcy, *The Saints of Ireland* (St. Paul, 1974); Eoin Neeson, *The Book of Irish Saints* (Cork, 1967).
13. For the revised Franciscan calendar: Marion A. Habig,

OFM, *The Franciscan Book of Saints,* rev. ed. (Chicago, 1979), pp. 975–979.

14. Cf. U.S. Catholic Conference, *Holy Days in the United States* (Washington, D.C., 1984), pp. 82–96.
15. Cf. Stephen Clissold, *The Saints of South America* (London, 1972).
16. Philip H. Pfatteicher, *Festivals and Commemorations* (Minneapolis, 1980), p. 16.
17. For the Lutherans: *The Church Year: Calendar and Lectionary* (Minneapolis, 1973), and *The Lutheran Book of Worship* (1978). For the Episcopal Church: *Lesser Feasts and Fasts,* rev. ed. (New York, 1973); *The Book of Common Prayer* (1979).

7. Unfinished Business

1. Cf. Timothy Ware, *The Orthodox Church* (New York, 1983), pp. 308–310.
2. Cf. Nicholas L. Chirovsky, *An Introduction to Ukrainian History* (New York, 1984), II, 78.
3. Cf. Denis-Boulet, *The Christian Calendar,* p. 109, note 1.
4. Cf. Adolf Adam, *The Liturgical Year,* p. 61. The quotation is from Luther's *On the Councils and the Church* (1539).
5. *Ibid.,* p. 60.
6. *Ibid.,* pp. 293–295.

Select Bibliography

Adam, Adolf. *The Liturgical Year* (New York, 1981).

Alberigo, Joseph et al., eds. *Conciliorum Oecumenicorum Decreta* (Bologna, 1973).

Attwater, Donald. *The Christian Churches of the East,* 2 vols. (Milwaukee, 1961–1962).

Barrois, Georges. *Scripture Readings in Orthodox Worship* (Crestwood, 1977).

Battifol, Pierre. *History of the Roman Breviary* (London, 1898).

Baumstark, Anton. *Comparative Liturgy* (Westminster, 1958).

Bettenson, Henry. *Documents of the Christian Church* (Oxford, 1947).

Bishop, Edmund. *Liturgica Historica* (Oxford, 1918).

Bonniwell, William R. *A History of the Dominican Liturgy* (New York, 1944).

Bradshaw, Paul F. *Daily Prayer in the Early Church* (New York, 1982).

Britt, Matthew. *The Hymns of the Breviary and Missal* (New York, 1952).

Brown, Peter. *The Cult of the Saints* (Chicago, 1981).

Bugnini, Annibale. *The Reform of the Liturgy 1948–1975* (Collegeville, 1990).

Byrnes, Aquinas. *The Hymns of the Dominican Missal and Breviary* (St. Louis, 1943).

Calendarium Romanum (Vatican City, 1969).

Chirovsky, Nicholas L. *An Introduction to Ukrainian History,* 2 vols. (New York, 1984).

Clissold, Stephen. *The Saints of South America* (London, 1972).

Cullmann, Oscar. *Early Christian Worship* (London, 1953).

———. *The Early Church* (London, 1956).

D'Arcy, Mary Ryan. *The Saints of Ireland* (St. Paul, 1974).

Davies, J.G., ed. *A Dictionary of Liturgy and Worship* (London, 1972).

———. *The Early Christian Church* (Grand Rapids, 1980).

Delehaye, Hippolyte. *The Legends of the Saints* (London, 1907).

Denis-Boulet, Noële M. *The Christian Calendar* (New York, 1960).

Dix, Gregory. *The Shape of the Liturgy* (London, 1945).

———. *The Apostolic Tradition,* reissued by Henry Chadwick (London, 1968).

Duchesne, Louis. *Christian Worship* (London, 1919).

Ehler, S.Z. and J.B. Morrall. *Church and State Through the Centuries* (Westminster, 1954).

Eisenhofer, L. and J. Lechner. *The Liturgy of the Roman Rite* (London, 1961).

Farmer, David Hugh. *The Oxford Dictionary of Saints* (Oxford, 1982).

Flannery, Austin, ed. *Vatican Council II,* rev. ed., 2 vols. (Northport, 1984).

Frere, Walter Howard. *Studies in Early Roman Liturgy,* Vol. I, *The Kalendar* (Oxford, 1930).

Habig, Marion A. *The Franciscan Book of Saints,* rev. ed. (Chicago, 1979).

Hampson, R.T. *Medii Aevi Kalendarium,* 2 vols. (London, 1841).

Heffernan, Thomas J. *Sacred Biography* (Oxford, 1988).

Hennecke, E. and W. Schneemelcher, eds. *New Testament Apocrypha,* 2 vols. (Philadelphia, 1963–1965).

Hopko, Thomas. *The Orthodox Faith,* Vol. 2, *Worship* (New York, 1976).

Jaubert, Annie. *The Date of the Last Supper* (Staten Island, 1965).

Jones, Cheslyn *et al. The Study of Liturgy* (New York, 1978).

Jungmann, Josef. *The Early Liturgy* (Notre Dame, 1959).

Kelly, J.N.D. *The Oxford Dictionary of Popes* (Oxford, 1986).

King, Archdale A. *Liturgies of the Religious Orders* (Milwaukee, 1955).

———. *Liturgies of the Primatial Sees* (Milwaukee, 1957).

———. *The Liturgy of the Roman Church* (Milwaukee, 1957).

———. *The Liturgies of the Past* (Milwaukee, 1959).

Kirch, C. *Enchiridion Fontium Historiae Ecclesiasticae Antiquae* (Barcelona, 1965).

Klauser, Theodor. *A Short History of the Western Liturgy* (Oxford, 1979).

Lake, Kirsopp, ed. *The Apostolic Fathers,* 2 vols. (London, 1912–1913).

Lamb, John Alexander. *The Psalms in Christian Worship* (London, 1962).

Lebreton, J. and J. Zeiller. *The History of the Primitive Church,* 2 vols. (New York, 1949).

Legg, J. Wickham, ed. *Breviarium Romanum a Francisco Cardinali Quignonio* (Cambridge, 1888).

Lietzmann, Hans. *A History of the Early Church,* 4 vols. (London, 1961).

Llewellyn, Peter. *Rome in the Dark Ages* (New York, 1971).

Loomis, Louis Ropes, ed. *The Book of the Popes* (New York, 1916).

Martimort, A.G. *et al. The Church at Prayer,* Vol. 4, *The Liturgy and Time* (Collegeville, 1986).

Maxwell, William D. *A History of Christian Worship* (Oxford, 1936).

McArthur, A.A. *The Evolution of the Christian Year* (London, 1953).

Neeson, Eoin. *The Book of Irish Saints* (Cork, 1967).

Nocent, Adrian. *The Liturgical Year,* 4 vols. (Collegeville, 1977).

O'Connell, J.B. *The Roman Martyrology* (Westminster, 1962).

O'Connor, Daniel W. *Peter in Rome* (New York, 1969).

Parsch, Pius. *The Church's Year of Grace,* 5 vols. (Collegeville, 1953–1959).

Pfatteicher, Philip H. *Festivals and Commemorations* (Minneapolis, 1980).

Pocknee, Cyril. *The Christian Altar* (London, 1963).

Quasten, Johannes. *Patrology,* 3 vols. (Westminster, 1950–1960). Vol. 4, ed. Angelo de Berardino (1986).

Raya, J. and J. de Vinck. *Byzantine Missal* (Birmingham, 1958).

———. *Byzantine Daily Worship* (Allendale, 1969).

Rordorf, Willi. *Sunday* (London, 1968).

Schmemann, Alexander. *Introduction to Liturgical Theology* (London, 1966).

Schroeder, H.J. *The Canons and Decrees of the Council of Trent* (Rockford, 1978), reprint of 1941 edition.

Sharp, Mary. *A Guide to the Churches of Rome* (London, 1966).

Taft, Robert. *Beyond East and West* (Washington, D.C., 1984).

———. *The Liturgy of the Hours in East and West* (Collegeville, 1986).

Thurston, H. and D. Attwater. *Butler's Lives of the Saints,* 4 vols. (New York, 1956).

Tylenda, Joseph N. *Jesuit Saints and Martyrs* (Chicago, 1984).

U.S. Catholic Conference. *Holy Days in the United States* (Washington, D.C., 1984).

———. *Norms Governing Liturgical Calendars* (Washington, D.C., 1984).

Van Dijk, S.J.P. and J. Hazelden Walker. *The Origins of the Modern Roman Liturgy* (London, 1960).

Vogel, Cyrille. *Medieval Liturgy: An Introduction to the Sources* (Washington, D.C., 1986).

Wainwright, Geoffrey. *Doxology* (Oxford, 1980).

Walsh, John Evangelist. *The Bones of Saint Peter* (Bungay, 1984).

Ware, Timothy. *The Orthodox Church* (Penguin Books, 1983).

Wegman, H. *Christian Worship in East and West* (New York, 1985).

Wilkinson, John, trans. *Egeria's Travels to the Holy Land* (Jerusalem, 1981).

APPENDIX A

The Old and New Roman Calendars

On the *left-hand* pages are the entries for the Roman calendar of 1954. Feasts printed in capital letters had the rank of double of the first or second class, or greater double. The first attempt to simplify the calendar was made in 1955, and included the following changes:

1. All vigils were abolished, except the vigils of Christmas, Ascension, Pentecost, Assumption, John the Baptist, Peter and Paul, and Lawrence.

2. All octaves were abolished, except the octaves of Christmas, Easter and Pentecost.

On the *right-hand* pages are the entries for the Roman calendar of 1969, with some later additions. Feasts printed in capital letters have the rank of solemnity or feast day. The remaining entries are either memorials or optional memorials.

January

1 CIRCUMCISION AND OCTAVE OF CHRISTMAS
Sunday between Circumcision and Epiphany: HOLY NAME
OF JESUS
2 Octave of Stephen the First Martyr
3 Octave of John the Apostle
4 Octave of the Holy Innocents
5 Vigil of the Epiphany. Com. of Pope Telesphorus
6 EPIPHANY
Sunday after Epiphany: HOLY FAMILY
7 Epiphany octave
8 Epiphany octave
9 Epiphany octave
10 Epiphany octave
11 Epiphany octave. Com. of Pope Hyginus
12 Epiphany octave
13 OCTAVE OF EPIPHANY
14 Hilary. Com. of Felix of Nola
15 Paul the First Hermit. Com. of Maurus
16 Pope Marcellus I
17 Anthony of Egypt
18 CHAIR OF PETER AT ROME. Com. of Prisca
19 Marius, Martha, Audifax and Abachum. Com. of Canute
20 Pope Fabian and Sebastian

21 Agnes
22 Vincent and Anastasius
23 Raymond of Peñafort. Com. of Emerentiana
24 Timothy
25 CONVERSION OF PAUL THE APOSTLE
26 Polycarp
27 John Chrysostom
28 Peter Nolasco. Com. of Agnes
29 Francis de Sales
30 Martina
31 John Bosco

January

1	OCTAVE OF CHRISTMAS SOLEMNITY OF MARY, MOTHER OF GOD	Solemnity
2	Basil the Great and Gregory Nazianzen	Memorial
3		
4		
5		
6	EPIPHANY	Solemnity
7	Raymond of Peñafort	
8		
9		
10		
11		
12		
13	Hilary	
14		
15		
16		
17	Anthony of Egypt	Memorial
18		
19		
20	Pope Fabian Sebastian	
21	Agnes	Memorial
22	Vincent	
23		
24	Francis de Sales	Memorial
25	CONVERSION OF PAUL THE APOSTLE	Feast
26	Timothy and Titus	Memorial
27	Angela Merici	
28	Thomas Aquinas	Memorial
29		
30		
31	John Bosco	Memorial

Sunday after January 6: BAPTISM OF THE LORD   Feast

155

February

1   Ignatius of Antioch
2   PURIFICATION OF MARY
3   Blase

4   Andrew Corsini
5   Agatha
6   Titus. Com. of Dorothy
7   Romuald
8   John of Matha
9   Cyril of Alexandria. Com. of Apollonia
10   Scholastica
11   APPARITION OF OUR LADY OF LOURDES
12   Seven Founders of the Servites
13
14   Valentine
15   Faustinus and Jovita
16
17
18   Simeon
19
20
21
22   CHAIR OF PETER AT ANTIOCH
23   Peter Damian. Com. of Vigil of Matthias the Apostle
24   MATTHIAS THE APOSTLE (February 25 in
       Leap Year)
25
26
27   Gabriel Possenti (February 28 in Leap Year)
28

156

February

1		
2	PRESENTATION OF THE LORD	Feast
3	Blase	
	Ansgar	
4		
5	Agatha	Memorial
6	Paul Miki and Companions	Memorial
7		
8	Jerome Emiliani	
9		
10	Scholastica	Memorial
11	Our Lady of Lourdes	
12		
13		
14	Cyril and Methodius	Memorial
15		
16		
17	Seven Holy Founders of the Servites	
18		
19		
20		
21	Peter Damian	
22	CHAIR OF PETER	Feast
23	Polycarp	Memorial
24		
25		
26		
27		
28		

March

```
 1
 2
 3
 4   Casimir. Com. of Pope Lucius I
 5
 6   Perpetua and Felicity
 7   Thomas Aquinas
 8   John of God
 9   Frances of Rome
10   Forty Martyrs
11
12   Pope Gregory the Great
13
14
15
16
17   Patrick
18   Cyril of Jerusalem
19   JOSEPH
20
21   BENEDICT
22
23
24   Gabriel the Archangel
25   ANNUNCIATION OF MARY
26
27   John of Damascus
28   John of Capistrano
29
30
31
```

Friday after Passion Sunday: OUR LADY OF SORROWS

March

1		
2		
3		
4	Casimir	
5		
6		
7	Perpetua and Felicity	Memorial
8	John of God	
9	Frances of Rome	
10		
11		
12		
13		
14		
15		
16		
17	Patrick	
18	Cyril of Jerusalem	
19	JOSEPH	Solemnity
20		
21		
22		
23	Turibius de Mongrovejo	
24		
25	ANNUNCIATION	Solemnity
26		
27		
28		
29		
30		
31		

April

```
1
2    Francis of Paola
3
4    Isidore of Seville
5    Vincent Ferrer
6
7
8
9
10
11   Pope Leo I
12
13   Hermenegild
14   Justin Martyr. Com. of Tiburtius, Valerian and Maximus
15
16
17   Pope Anicetus
18
19
20
21   Anselm of Canterbury
22   Soter and Caius
23   George
24   Fidelis of Sigmaringen
25   MARK THE EVANGELIST
26   Popes Cletus and Marcellinus
27   Peter Canisius
28   Paul of the Cross. Com. of Vitalis
29   Peter Martyr of Verona
30   Catherine of Siena
```

Third Wednesday after Easter: SOLEMNITY OF ST. JOSEPH
Fourth Wednesday after Easter: OCTAVE OF ST. JOSEPH

April

1		
2	Francis of Paola	
3		
4	Isidore of Seville	
5	Vincent Ferrer	
6		
7	John Baptist de la Salle	Memorial
8		
9		
10		
11	Stanislaus	Memorial
12		
13	Pope Martin I	
14		
15		
16		
17		
18		
19		
20		
21	Anselm of Canterbury	
22		
23	George	
24	Fidelis of Sigmaringen	
25	MARK THE EVANGELIST	Feast
26		
27		
28	Peter Chanel	
29	Catherine of Siena	Memorial
30	Pope Pius V	

May

1 PHILIP AND JAMES THE APOSTLES*
2 Athanasius
3 FINDING OF THE HOLY CROSS. Com. of Pope Alexander I, Eventius, Theodulus and Juvenal
4 Monica
5 Pope Pius V
6 JOHN THE APOSTLE BEFORE THE LATIN GATE
7 Stanislaus
8 APPARITION OF MICHAEL THE ARCHANGEL
9 Gregory of Nazianzus
10 Antoninus. Com. of Gordian and Epimachus
11
12 Nereus, Achilleus, Domitilla and Pancras

13 Robert Bellarmine
14 Boniface of Tarsus
15 John Baptist de la Salle
16 Ubaldus
17 Paschal Baylon
18 Venantius
19 Pope Celestine V. Com. of Pudentiana
20 Bernardine of Siena
21
22
23
24
25 Pope Gregory VII. Com. of Pope Urban I

26 Philip Neri. Com. of Pope Eleutherius
27 Bede the Venerable. Com. of Pope John I
28 Augustine of Canterbury
29 Mary Magdalene de Pazzi
30 Pope Felix I
31 Angela Merici. Com. of Petronilla**

---

* In 1955 the feast of Joseph the Worker was assigned to May 1; the feast of Sts. Philip and James was transferred to May 11.
** In 1954 the feast of the Queenship of Mary was assigned to May 31; the feast of St. Angela was transferred to June 1.

May

1	Joseph the Worker	
2	Athanasius	Memorial
3	PHILIP AND JAMES THE APOSTLES	Feast
4		
5		
6		
7		
8		
9		
10		
11		
12	Nereus and Achilleus	
	Pancras	
13		
14	MATTHIAS THE APOSTLE	Feast
15		
16		
17		
18	Pope John I	
19		
20	Bernardine of Siena	
21		
22		
23		
24		
25	Bede the Venerable	
	Pope Gregory VII	
	Mary Magdalene de Pazzi	
26	Philip Neri	Memorial
27	Augustine of Canterbury	
28		
29		
30		
31	VISITATION	Feast

First Sunday after Pentecost: TRINITY SUNDAY	Solemnity
Thursday after Trinity Sunday: CORPUS CHRISTI	Solemnity
Friday after Pentecost II: SACRED HEART OF JESUS	Solemnity

June

```
 1
 2  Marcellinus, Peter and Erasmus
 3
 4  Francis Caracciolo
 5  Boniface
 6  Norbert
 7
 8
 9  Primus and Felician
10  Margaret of Scotland
11  BARNABAS THE APOSTLE
12  John of Sahagun. Com. of Basilides, Cyrinus, Nabor and Nazarius
13  Anthony of Padua
14  Basil
15  Vitus, Modestus and Crescentia
16
17
18  Ephrem the Syrian. Com. of Mark and Marcellian
19  Juliana Falconieri. Com. of Gervase and Protase
20  Pope Silverius
21  Aloysius Gonzaga
22  Paulinus of Nola

23  Vigil of John the Baptist
24  BIRTH OF JOHN THE BAPTIST
25  William of Vercelli. Com. of octave of John the Baptist
26  John and Paul. Com. of octave of John the Baptist
27  Octave of John the Baptist
28  Irenaeus of Lyons. Com. of octave and vigil of Peter and Paul
29  PETER AND PAUL THE APOSTLES
30  COMMEMORATION OF PAUL THE APOSTLE. Com. of octave
```

June

1	Justin Martyr	Memorial
2	Marcellinus and Peter	
3	Charles Lwanga and Companions	Memorial
4		
5	Boniface	Memorial
6	Norbert	
7		
8		
9	Ephrem the Syrian	
10		
11	Barnabas the Apostle	Memorial
12		
13	Anthony of Padua	Memorial
14		
15		
16		
17		
18		
19	Romuald	
20		
21	Aloysius Gonzaga	Memorial
22	Paulinus of Nola	
	John Fisher and Thomas More	
23		
24	BIRTH OF JOHN THE BAPTIST	Solemnity
25		
26		
27	Cyril of Alexandria	
28	Irenaeus of Lyons	Memorial
29	PETER AND PAUL THE APOSTLES	Solemnity
30	First Martyrs of the Church of Rome	

July

1   PRECIOUS BLOOD. Com. of octave of John the Baptist
2   VISITATION. Com. of Processus and Martinian
3   Pope Leo II. Com. of octave of Peter and Paul
4   Octave of Peter and Paul
5   Anthony Zaccaria. Com. of octave of Peter and Paul
6   OCTAVE OF PETER AND PAUL
7   Cyril and Methodius
8   Elizabeth of Portugal
9
10   Seven Brothers, and Rufina and Secunda
11   Pope Pius I
12   John Gualbert. Com. of Nabor and Felix
13   Pope Anacletus
14   Bonaventure
15   Emperor Henry II
16   OUR LADY OF MOUNT CARMEL
17   Alexis
18   Camillus de Lellis. Com. of Symphorosa and Her Seven Sons
19   Vincent de Paul
20   Jerome Emiliani. Com. of Margaret
21   Praxedes
22   Mary Magdalene
23   Apollinaris. Com. of Liborius
24   Vigil of James the Apostle. Com. of Christina
25   JAMES THE APOSTLE. Com. of Christopher
26   ANN
27   Panteleimon
28   Nazarius and Celsus, Pope Victor I and Pope
     Innocent I
29   Martha. Com. of Pope Felix II, Simplicius, Faustinus and Beatrice
30   Abdon and Sennen
31   IGNATIUS OF LOYOLA

July

1		
2		
3	THOMAS THE APOSTLE	Feast
4	Elizabeth of Portugal	
5	Anthony Zaccaria	
6	Maria Goretti	
7		
8		
9		
10		
11	Benedict	Memorial
12		
13	Emperor Henry II	
14	Camillus de Lellis	
15	Bonaventure	Memorial
16	Our Lady of Mount Carmel	
17		
18		
19		
20		
21	Lawrence of Brindisi	
22	Mary Magdalene	Memorial
23	Bridget of Sweden	
24		
25	JAMES THE APOSTLE	Feast
26	Joachim and Ann	Memorial
27		
28		
29	Martha	Memorial
30	Peter Chrysologus	
31	Ignatius of Loyola	Memorial

August

1 PETER IN CHAINS. Com. of the Maccabees
2 Alphonsus Liguori. Com. of Pope Stephen I
3 Finding of Stephen the First Martyr
4 DOMINIC
5 OUR LADY OF THE SNOWS
6 TRANSFIGURATION. Com. of Pope Sixtus II, Felicissimus and Agapitus
7 Cajetan. Com. of Donatus

8 Cyriacus, Largus and Smaragdus
9 John Vianney. Com. of vigil and Romanus
10 LAWRENCE
11 Tiburtius and Susanna
12 Clare of Assisi
13 Hippolytus and Cassian
14 Vigil of the Assumption. Com. of Eusebius
15 ASSUMPTION
16 JOACHIM
17 Hyacinth. Com. of octaves of Assumption and Lawrence
18 Assumption octave. Com. of Agapitus
19 John Eudes. Com. of Assumption octave
20 Bernard. Com. of Assumption octave
21 Jane Frances de Chantal. Com. of Assumption octave
22 IMMACULATE HEART OF MARY. Com. of Timothy, Hippolytus and Symphorian
23 Philip Benizi. Com. of vigil of Bartholomew the Apostle
24 BARTHOLOMEW THE APOSTLE
25 King Louis IX

26 Pope Zephyrinus
27 Joseph Calasanz
28 Augustine. Com. of Hermes
29 BEHEADING OF JOHN THE BAPTIST. Com. of Sabina
30 Rose of Lima. Com. of Felix and Adauctus
31 Raymond Nonnatus

August

1	Alphonsus Liguori	Memorial
2	Eusebius of Vercelli	
3		
4	John Vianney	Memorial
5	Dedication of St. Mary Major	
6	TRANSFIGURATION	Feast
7	Pope Sixtus II and Companions	
	Cajetan	
8	Dominic	Memorial
9		
10	LAWRENCE	Feast
11	Clare of Assisi	Memorial
12		
13	Pope Pontian and Hippolytus	
14	Maximilian Kolbe	Memorial
15	ASSUMPTION	Solemnity
16	King Stephen of Hungary	
17		
18		
19	John Eudes	
20	Bernard	Memorial
21	Pope Pius X	Memorial
22	Queenship of Mary	Memorial
23	Rose of Lima	
24	BARTHOLOMEW THE APOSTLE	Feast
25	King Louis IX	
	Joseph Calasanz	
26		
27	Monica	Memorial
28	Augustine	Memorial
29	Beheading of John the Baptist	Memorial
30		
31		

September

1 Giles. Com. of the Twelve Brothers
2 King Stephen of Hungary
3
4
5 Lawrence Justinian
6
7
8 BIRTH OF MARY. Com. of Hadrian
9 Gorgonius
10 Nicholas of Tolentine
11 Protus and Hyacinth
12 HOLY NAME OF MARY
13
14 EXALTATION OF THE HOLY CROSS
15 OUR LADY OF SORROWS. Com. of Nicomedes
16 Pope Cornelius and Cyprian. Com. of Euphemia, Lucy and Geminianus
17 Stigmata of Francis of Assisi
18 Joseph of Cupertino
19 Januarius and Companions
20 Eustace and Companions. Com. of vigil of Matthew the Apostle
21 MATTHEW THE APOSTLE
22 Thomas of Villanova. Com. of Maurice and Companions
23 Pope Linus. Com. of Thecla
24 OUR LADY OF RANSOM
25
26 Cyprian and Justina
27 Cosmas and Damian
28 Wenceslaus

29 MICHAEL THE ARCHANGEL
30 Jerome

September

1		
2		
3	Pope Gregory the Great	Memorial
4		
5		
6		
7		
8	BIRTH OF MARY	Feast
9		
10		
11		
12		
13	John Chrysostom	Memorial
14	TRIUMPH OF THE HOLY CROSS	Feast
15	Our Lady of Sorrows	Memorial
16	Pope Cornelius and Cyprian	Memorial
17	Robert Bellarmine	
18		
19	Januarius	
20	Andrew Kim, Paul Chong and Companions	Memorial
21	MATTHEW THE APOSTLE	Feast
22		
23		
24		
25		
26	Cosmas and Damian	
27	Vincent de Paul	Memorial
28	Wenceslaus	
	Lawrence Ruiz and Companions	
29	MICHAEL, GABRIEL AND RAPHAEL THE ARCHANGELS	Feast
30	Jerome	Memorial

171

October

1   Remigius
2   GUARDIAN ANGELS
3   Theresa of the Child Jesus
4   FRANCIS OF ASSISI
5   Placid and Companions
6   Bruno
7   HOLY ROSARY. Com. of Pope Mark, Sergius, Bacchus, Marcellus and Apuleius
8   Bridget of Sweden
9   John Leonardi. Com. of Denis, Rusticus and Eleutherius

10   Francis Borgia
11   MATERNITY OF MARY
12
13   King Edward the Confessor
14   Pope Callistus I
15   Teresa of Avila
16   Hedwig

17   Margaret Mary Alacoque
18   LUKE THE EVANGELIST
19   Peter of Alcantara

20   John of Kanty
21   Hilarion. Com. of Ursula and Companions
22
23
24   RAPHAEL THE ARCHANGEL
25   Chrysanthus and Daria
26   Pope Evaristus
27   Vigil of Simon and Jude the Apostles
28   SIMON AND JUDE THE APOSTLES
29
30
31   Vigil of All Saints

Last Sunday in October: CHRIST THE KING

October

1	Theresa of the Child Jesus	Memorial
2	Guardian Angels	Memorial
3		
4	Francis of Assisi	Memorial
5		
6	Bruno	
7	Our Lady of the Rosary	Memorial
8		
9	Denis and Companions	
	John Leonardi	
10		
11		
12		
13		
14	Pope Callistus I	
15	Teresa of Jesus	Memorial
16	Hedwig	
	Margaret Mary Alacoque	
17	Ignatius of Antioch	Memorial
18	LUKE THE EVANGELIST	Feast
19	Isaac Jogues and Companions	
	Paul of the Cross	
20		
21		
22		
23	John of Capistrano	
24	Anthony Claret	
25		
26		
27		
28	SIMON AND JUDE THE APOSTLES	Feast
29		
30		
31		

November

1 ALL SAINTS
2 All Souls
3 All Saints octave
4 Charles Borromeo. Com. of octave and Vitalis and Agricola
5 All Saints octave
6 All Saints octave
7 All Saints octave
8 OCTAVE OF ALL SAINTS. Com. of Four Crowned Martyrs
9 DEDICATION OF BASILICA OF OUR SAVIOUR. Com.
   of Theodore
10 Andrew Avellino. Com. of Tryphon, Respicius and Nympha
11 Martin of Tours. Com. of Mennas
12 Pope Martin I
13 Didacus
14 Josaphat
15 Albert the Great
16 Gertrude

17 Gregory the Wonderworker
18 DEDICATION OF BASILICAS OF PETER
    AND PAUL
19 Elizabeth of Hungary. Com. of Pope Pontian
20 Felix of Valois
21 PRESENTATION OF MARY
22 Cecilia
23 Pope Clement I. Com. of Felicity

24 John of the Cross. Com. of Chrysogonus
25 Catherine of Alexandria
26 Sylvester Gozzolini. Com. of Peter of Alexandria
27
28
29 Vigil of Andrew the Apostle. Com. of Saturninus
30 ANDREW THE APOSTLE

November

1	ALL SAINTS	Solemnity
2	ALL SOULS	
3	Martin de Porres	
4	Charles Borromeo	Memorial
5		
6		
7		
8		
9	DEDICATION OF THE LATERAN BASILICA	Feast
10	Pope Leo the Great	Memorial
11	Martin of Tours	Memorial
12	Josaphat	Memorial
13		
14		
15	Albert the Great	
16	Margaret of Scotland	
	Gertrude	
17	Elizabeth of Hungary	Memorial
18	Dedication of Basilicas of Peter and Paul	
19		
20		
21	Presentation of Mary	Memorial
22	Cecilia	Memorial
23	Pope Clement I	
	Columban	
24	Andrew Dung-Lac and Companions	Memorial
25		
26		
27		
28		
29		
30	ANDREW THE APOSTLE	Feast

Last Sunday of the year: CHRIST THE KING   Solemnity

December

1
2 Bibiana
3 FRANCIS XAVIER
4 Peter Chrysologus. Com. of Barbara
5 Sabbas
6 Nicholas
7 Ambrose. Com. of vigil of Immaculate Conception
8 IMMACULATE CONCEPTION
9 Immaculate Conception octave
10 Immaculate Conception octave. Com. of Pope Melchiades
11 Pope Damasus I. Com. of Immaculate Conception octave
12 Immaculate Conception octave
13 Lucy. Com. of Immaculate Conception octave
14 Immaculate Conception octave
15 OCTAVE OF IMMACULATE CONCEPTION
16 Eusebius
17
18
19
20 Vigil of Thomas the Apostle
21 THOMAS THE APOSTLE
22
23
24 Vigil of Christmas
25 CHRISTMAS. Com. of Anastasia
26 STEPHEN THE FIRST MARTYR. Com. of Christmas octave
27 JOHN THE APOSTLE. Com. of Christmas octave
28 HOLY INNOCENTS. Com. of Christmas octave
29 Thomas Becket. Com. of Christmas octave
30 Christmas octave
31 Pope Sylvester I. Com. of Christmas octave

December

1		
2		
3	Francis Xavier	Memorial
4	John of Damascus	
5		
6	Nicholas	
7	Ambrose	Memorial
8	IMMACULATE CONCEPTION	Solemnity
9		
10		
11	Pope Damasus I	
12	Jane Frances de Chantal	
13	Lucy	Memorial
14	John of the Cross	Memorial
15		
16		
17		
18		
19		
20		
21	Peter Canisius	
22		
23	John of Kanty	
24		
25	CHRISTMAS	Solemnity
26	STEPHEN THE FIRST MARTYR	Feast
27	JOHN THE APOSTLE	Feast
28	HOLY INNOCENTS	Feast
29	Thomas Becket	
30		
31	Pope Sylvester I	

Sunday within the Octave of Christmas: HOLY FAMILY — Feast

177

APPENDIX B

National Calendars

National Calendar for the United States

Jan. 4	Elizabeth Ann Seton	Memorial
5	John Neumann	Memorial
6	André Bessette	
Mar. 3	Katherine Drexel	
May 15	Isidore the Farmer	
July 1	Junipero Serra	
4	Independence Day	
14	Kateri Tekakwitha	Memorial
Sep. 9	Peter Claver	Memorial
Oct. 6	Marie Rose Durocher	
19	Isaac Jogues and Companions	Memorial
Nov. 13	Frances Xavier Cabrini	Memorial
18	Rose Philippine Duchesne	
Fourth Thursday	Thanksgiving Day	
Dec. 12	Our Lady of Guadalupe	Feast

National Calendar for Canada

Jan. 6	André Bessette	
12	Marguerite Bourgeoys	Memorial
Mar. 19	Joseph (Principal Patron)	Solemnity
Apr. 26	Our Lady of Good Counsel	
30	Marie of the Incarnation	
May 4	Marie-Leonie Paradis	

6	Francis de Montmorency Laval	
24	Louis Moreau	
July 14	Kateri Tekakwitha	Memorial
Oct. 6	Marie-Rose Durocher	
16	Marguerite d'Youville	
19	John de Brebeuf, Isaac Jogues and Companions	Memorial

National Calendar for Ireland

Feb. 1	Brigid	Feast
Mar. 17	Patrick (Patron of Ireland)	Solemnity
June 9	Columba (Colum Cille)	Feast
July 1	Oliver Plunkett	Feast
Nov. 6	All Saints of Ireland	Feast
23	Columban	Feast

National Calendar for England

Mar. 1	David (Patron of Wales)	Feast
17	Patrick (Patron of Ireland)	Feast
Apr. 21	Anselm of Canterbury	Memorial
23	George (Patron of England)	Feast
May 4	Beatified Martyrs of England and Wales	Feast
25	Bede the Venerable	Memorial
27	Augustine of Canterbury, Apostle of England	Feast
June 20	Alban, Protomartyr of England	Memorial
22	John Fisher and Thomas More	Feast
Aug. 26	Dominic Barberi	

Sep. 3	Pope Gregory the Great, Apostle of the English	Feast
24	Our Lady of Ransom	Memorial
Oct. 13	King Edward the Confessor	Memorial
25	Cuthbert Mayne and Companions (Forty Martyrs)	Feast
Dec. 29	Thomas à Becket, Patron of the Pastoral Clergy	Feast

National Calendar for Scotland

Jan. 13	Kentigern	Memorial
Mar. 10	John Ogilvie	Feast
17	Patrick	Feast
June 9	Columba	Memorial
Aug. 26	Ninian	Memorial
Nov. 16	Margaret (Secondary Patron of Scotland)	Feast
30	Andrew the Apostle (Principal Patron of Scotland)	Solemnity

National Calendar for Wales

Feb. 9	Teilo	
Mar. 1	David (Patron of Wales)	Solemnity
17	Patrick (Patron of Ireland)	Feast
Apr. 20	Beuno	
23	George (Patron of England)	Feast
May 4	Beatified Martyrs of England and Wales	
5	Asaph	

June 20	Alban, Julius and Aaron, Protomartyrs of Britain	Memorial
22	John Fisher and Thomas More	Memorial
July 12	John Jones	
23	Philip Evans and John Lloyd	
Aug. 3	Germanus of Auxerre	
26	David Lewis	
Sep. 11	Deiniol	
Oct. 16	Richard Gwyn	
25	The Six Welsh Martyrs and Companions	Feast
Nov. 3	Winefride	
6	Illtud	
8	All Saints of Wales	Feast
14	Dyfrig	
Dec. 10	John Roberts	

National Calendar for Australia

Mar. 17	Patrick, Patron of Ireland	Solemnity
Apr. 28	Peter Chanel	Memorial
May 24	Our Lady Help of Christians	Solemnity
Oct. 1	Theresa of the Child Jesus	Feast
Dec. 3	Francis Xavier	Feast

Index

The saints of the church are listed under their Christian names.